MySQL
Tutorial

-The ultimate Beginners Guide-

Understand the Basics-to-advanced concepts of MySQL languages

Table of Contents

MySQL Tutorial iv

Audience v

Prerequisites vi

MySQL - Introduction .... - 1 -

MySQL - Installation .... - 4 -

    Use the mysqladmin Utility to Obtain Server Status .... - 6 -

    Execute simple SQL commands using the MySQL Client .... - 7 -

MySQL - Administration .... - 9 -

MySQL - PHP Syntax .... - 14 -

MySQL - Connection .... - 16 -

MySQL - Create Database .... - 20 -

Drop MySQL Database .... - 23 -

Selecting MySQL Database .... - 26 -

MySQL - Data Types .... - 28 -

Create MySQL Tables .... - 32 -

Drop MySQL Tables .... - 35 -

MySQL - Insert Query .... - 37 -

MySQL - Select Query .... - 42 -

MySQL - WHERE Clause .... - 49 -

MySQL - UPDATE Query .... - 54 -

MySQL - DELETE Query .... - 57 -

MySQL - LIKE Clause .... - 60 -

MySQL - Sorting Results .... - 63 -

Using MySQl Joins .... - 66 -

Handling MySQL NULL Values .... - 70 -
MySQL - Regexps .... - 75 -
MySQL - Transactions .... - 77 -
MySQL - ALTER Command .... - 81 -
MySQL - INDEXES .... - 86 -
MySQL - Temporary Tables .... - 89 -
MySQL - Clone Tables .... - 92 -
MySQL - Database Info .... - 94 -
    PERL Example .... - 95 -
    PHP Example .... - 96 -
Using MySQL Sequences .... - 98 -
MySQL - Handling Duplicates .... - 102 -
MySQL - and SQL Injection .... - 106 -
MySQL - Database Export .... - 108 -
MySQL - Database Import - Recovery Methods .... - 113 -

MySQL Tutorial

MySQL is the most popular Open Source Relational SQL Database Management System. MySQL is one of the best RDBMS being used for developing various web-based software applications. MySQL is developed, marketed and supported by MySQL AB, which is a Swedish company. This tutorial will give you a quick start to MySQL and make you comfortable with MySQL programming.

Audience

This tutorial is prepared for the beginners to help them understand the basics-to-advanced concepts related to MySQL languages.

Prerequisites

Before you start doing practice with various types of examples given in this tutorial, it is being assumed that you are already aware about what a database is, especially an RDBMS and what is a computer programming language.

MySQL - Introduction

What is a Database?

A database is a separate application that stores a collection of data. Each database has one or more distinct APIs for creating, accessing, managing, searching and replicating the data it holds.

Other kinds of data stores can also be used, such as files on the file system or large hash tables in memory but data fetching and writing would not be so fast and easy with those type of systems.

Nowadays, we use relational database management systems (RDBMS) to store and manage huge volume of data. This is called relational database because all the data is stored into different tables and relations are established using primary keys or other keys known as Foreign Keys.

A Relational DataBase Management System (RDBMS) is a software that –

- Enables you to implement a database with tables, columns and indexes.
- Guarantees the Referential Integrity between rows of various tables.
- Updates the indexes automatically.
- Interprets an SQL query and combines information from various tables.

RDBMS Terminology

Before we proceed to explain the MySQL database system, let us revise a few definitions related to the database.

- Database – A database is a collection of tables, with related data.
- Table – A table is a matrix with data. A table in a database looks like a simple spreadsheet.

- Column – One column (data element) contains data of one and the same kind, for example the column postcode.
- Row – A row (= tuple, entry or record) is a group of related data, for example the data of one subscription.
- Redundancy – Storing data twice, redundantly to make the system faster.
- Primary Key – A primary key is unique. A key value can not occur twice in one table. With a key, you can only find one row.
- Foreign Key – A foreign key is the linking pin between two tables.
- Compound Key – A compound key (composite key) is a key that consists of multiple columns, because one column is not sufficiently unique.
- Index – An index in a database resembles an index at the back of a book.
- Referential Integrity – Referential Integrity makes sure that a foreign key value always points to an existing row.

MySQL Database

MySQL is a fast, easy-to-use RDBMS being used for many small and big businesses. MySQL is developed, marketed and supported by MySQL AB, which is a Swedish company. MySQL is becoming so popular because of many good reasons –

- MySQL is released under an open-source license. So you have nothing to pay to use it.
- MySQL is a very powerful program in its own right. It handles a large subset of the functionality of the most expensive and powerful database packages.
- MySQL uses a standard form of the well-known SQL data language.
- MySQL works on many operating systems and with many languages including PHP, PERL, C, C++, JAVA, etc.
- MySQL works very quickly and works well even with large data sets.
- MySQL is very friendly to PHP, the most appreciated language for web development.

- MySQL supports large databases, up to 50 million rows or more in a table. The default file size limit for a table is 4GB, but you can increase this (if your operating system can handle it) to a theoretical limit of 8 million terabytes (TB).
- MySQL is customizable. The open-source GPL license allows programmers to modify the MySQL software to fit their own specific environments.
-

Before You Begin

Before you begin this tutorial, you should have a basic knowledge of the information covered in our PHP and HTML tutorials.

This tutorial focuses heavily on using MySQL in a PHP environment. Many examples given in this tutorial will be useful for PHP Programmers.

MySQL - Installation

All downloads for MySQL are located at MySQL Downloads. Pick the version number of MySQL Community Server which is required along with the platform you will be running it on.

Installing MySQL on Linux/UNIX

The recommended way to install MySQL on a Linux system is via RPM. MySQL AB makes the following RPMs available for download on its website −

- MySQL − The MySQL database server manages the databases and tables, controls user access and processes the SQL queries.
- MySQL-client − MySQL client programs, which make it possible to connect to and interact with the server.
- MySQL-devel − Libraries and header files that come in handy when compiling other programs that use MySQL.
- MySQL-shared − Shared libraries for the MySQL client.
- MySQL-bench − Benchmark and performance testing tools for the MySQL database server.

The MySQL RPMs listed here are all built on a SuSE Linux system, but they will usually work on other Linux variants with no difficulty.

Now, you will need to adhere to the steps given below, to proceed with the installation −

- Login to the system using the root user.
- Switch to the directory containing the RPMs.

- Install the MySQL database server by executing the following command. Remember to replace the filename in italics with the file name of your RPM.

[root@host]# rpm -i MySQL-5.0.9-0.i386.rpm

The above command takes care of installing the MySQL server, creating a user of MySQL, creating necessary configuration and starting the MySQL server automatically.

You can find all the MySQL related binaries in /usr/bin and /usr/sbin. All the tables and databases will be created in the /var/lib/mysql directory.

- The following code box has an optional but recommended step to install the remaining RPMs in the same manner –

[root@host]# rpm -i MySQL-client-5.0.9-0.i386.rpm
[root@host]# rpm -i MySQL-devel-5.0.9-0.i386.rpm
[root@host]# rpm -i MySQL-shared-5.0.9-0.i386.rpm
[root@host]# rpm -i MySQL-bench-5.0.9-0.i386.rpm

Installing MySQL on Windows

The default installation on any version of Windows is now much easier than it used to be, as MySQL now comes neatly packaged with an installer. Simply download the installer package, unzip it anywhere and run the setup.exe file.

The default installer setup.exe will walk you through the trivial process and by default will install everything under C:\mysql.

Test the server by firing it up from the command prompt the first time. Go to the location of the mysqld server which is probably C:\mysql\bin, and type –

mysqld.exe --console

NOTE – If you are on NT, then you will have to use mysqld-nt.exe instead of mysqld.exe

If all went well, you will see some messages about startup and InnoDB. If not, you may have a permissions issue. Make sure that the directory that holds your data is accessible to whatever user (probably MySQL) the database processes run under.

MySQL will not add itself to the start menu, and there is no particularly nice GUI way to stop the server either. Therefore, if you tend to start the server by double clicking the mysqld executable, you should remember to halt the process by hand by using mysqladmin, Task List, Task Manager, or other Windows-specific means.

Verifying MySQL Installation

After MySQL, has been successfully installed, the base tables have been initialized and the server has been started: you can verify that everything is working as it should be via some simple tests.

Use the mysqladmin Utility to Obtain Server Status

Use mysqladmin binary to check the server version. This binary would be available in /usr/bin on linux and in C:\mysql\bin on windows.

[root@host]# mysqladmin --version

It will produce the following result on Linux. It may vary depending on your installation −

mysqladmin Ver 8.23 Distrib 5.0.9-0, for redhat-linux-gnu on i386

If you do not get such a message, then there may be some problem in your installation and you would need some help to fix it.

Execute simple SQL commands using the MySQL Client

You can connect to your MySQL server through the MySQL client and by using the mysql command. At this moment, you do not need to give any password as by default it will be set as blank.

You can just use following command –

[root@host]# mysql

It should be rewarded with a mysql> prompt. Now, you are connected to the MySQL server and you can execute all the SQL commands at the mysql> prompt as follows –

```
mysql> SHOW DATABASES;
+----------+
| Database |
+----------+
|  mysql  |
|  test   |
+----------+
2 rows in set (0.13 sec)
```

Post-installation Steps

MySQL ships with a blank password for the root MySQL user. As soon as you have successfully installed the database and the client, you need to set a root password as given in the following code block –

[root@host]# mysqladmin -u root password "new_password";

Now to make a connection to your MySQL server, you would have to use the following command –

[root@host]# mysql -u root -p
Enter password:*******

UNIX users will also want to put your MySQL directory in your PATH, so you won't have to keep typing out the full path everytime you want to use the command-line client.

For bash, it would be something like –

export PATH = $PATH:/usr/bin:/usr/sbin

Running MySQL at Boot Time

If you want to run the MySQL server at boot time, then make sure you have the following entry in the /etc/rc.local file.

/etc/init.d/mysqld start

Also,you should have the mysqld binary in the /etc/init.d/ directory.

MySQL - Administration

Running and Shutting down MySQL Server

First check if your MySQL server is running or not. You can use the following command to check it −

ps -ef | grep mysqld

If your MySql is running, then you will see mysqld process listed out in your result. If server is not running, then you can start it by using the following command −

root@host# cd /usr/bin
./safe_mysqld &

Now, if you want to shut down an already running MySQL server, then you can do it by using the following command −

root@host# cd /usr/bin
./mysqladmin -u root -p shutdown
Enter password: ******

Setting Up a MySQL User Account

For adding a new user to MySQL, you just need to add a new entry to the user table in the database mysql.

The following program is an example of adding a new user guest with SELECT, INSERT and UPDATE privileges with the password guest123; the SQL query is –

```
root@host# mysql -u root -p
Enter password:*******
mysql> use mysql;
Database changed

mysql> INSERT INTO user
     (host, user, password,
      select_priv, insert_priv, update_priv)
     VALUES ('localhost', 'guest',
      PASSWORD('guest123'), 'Y', 'Y', 'Y');
Query OK, 1 row affected (0.20 sec)

mysql> FLUSH PRIVILEGES;
Query OK, 1 row affected (0.01 sec)

mysql> SELECT host, user, password FROM user WHERE user = 'guest';
+-----------+---------+------------------+
| host      | user    | password         |
+-----------+---------+------------------+
| localhost | guest   | 6f8c114b58f2ce9e |
+-----------+---------+------------------+
1 row in set (0.00 sec)
```

When adding a new user, remember to encrypt the new password using PASSWORD() function provided by MySQL. As you can see in the above example, the password mypass is encrypted to 6f8c114b58f2ce9e.

Notice the FLUSH PRIVILEGES statement. This tells the server to reload the grant tables. If you don't use it, then you won't be able to connect to MySQL using the new user account at least until the server is rebooted.

You can also specify other privileges to a new user by setting the values of following columns in user table to 'Y' when executing the INSERT query or you can update them later using UPDATE query.

- Select_priv
- Insert_priv
- Update_priv
- Delete_priv
- Create_priv
- Drop_priv
- Reload_priv
- Shutdown_priv
- Process_priv
- File_priv
- Grant_priv
- References_priv
- Index_priv
- Alter_priv

Another way of adding user account is by using GRANT SQL command. The following example will add user zara with password zara123 for a particular database, which is named as TUTORIALS.

```
root@host# mysql -u root -p password;
Enter password:*******
mysql> use mysql;
Database changed

mysql> GRANT SELECT,INSERT,UPDATE,DELETE,CREATE,DROP
   -> ON TUTORIALS.*
   -> TO 'zara'@'localhost'
   -> IDENTIFIED BY 'zara123';
```

This will also create an entry in the MySQL database table called as user.

NOTE – MySQL does not terminate a command until you give a semi colon (;) at the end of the SQL command.

The /etc/my.cnf File Configuration

In most of the cases, you should not touch this file. By default, it will have the following entries –

[mysqld]
datadir = /var/lib/mysql
socket = /var/lib/mysql/mysql.sock

[mysql.server]
user = mysql
basedir = /var/lib

[safe_mysqld]
err-log = /var/log/mysqld.log
pid-file = /var/run/mysqld/mysqld.pid

Here, you can specify a different directory for the error log, otherwise you should not change any entry in this table.

Administrative MySQL Command

Here is the list of the important MySQL commands, which you will use time to time to work with MySQL database –

- USE Databasename – This will be used to select a database in the MySQL workarea.
- SHOW DATABASES – Lists out the databases that are accessible by the MySQL DBMS.
- SHOW TABLES – Shows the tables in the database once a database has been selected with the use command.

- SHOW COLUMNS FROM *tablename:* Shows the attributes, types of attributes, key information, whether NULL is permitted, defaults, and other information for a table.
- SHOW INDEX FROM tablename – Presents the details of all indexes on the table, including the PRIMARY KEY.
- SHOW TABLE STATUS LIKE tablename\G – Reports details of the MySQL DBMS performance and statistics.

In the next chapter, we will discuss regarding how PHP Syntax is used in MySQL.

MySQL - PHP Syntax

MySQL works very well in combination of various programming languages like PERL, C, C++, JAVA and PHP. Out of these languages, PHP is the most popular one because of its web application development capabilities.

This tutorial focuses heavily on using MySQL in a PHP environment. If you are interested in MySQL with PERL, then you can consider reading the PERLTutorial.

PHP provides various functions to access the MySQL database and to manipulate the data records inside the MySQL database. You would require to call the PHP functions in the same way you call any other PHP function.

The PHP functions for use with MySQL have the following general format −

mysql_*function*(value,value,...);

The second part of the function name is specific to the function, usually a word that describes what the function does. The following are two of the functions, which we will use in our tutorial −

mysqli_connect($connect);
mysqli_query($connect,"SQL statement");

The following example shows a generic syntax of PHP to call any MySQL function.

```html
<html>
  <head>
    <title>PHP with MySQL</title>
  </head>
  <body>
    <?php
      $retval = mysql_function(value, [value,...]);
      if( !$retval ) {
        die ( "Error: a related error message" );
      }
      // Otherwise MySQL or PHP Statements
    ?>
  </body>
</html>
```

Starting from the next chapter, we will see all the important MySQL functionality along with PHP.

MySQL - Connection

MySQL Connection Using MySQL Binary

You can establish the MySQL database using the mysql binary at the command prompt.

Example

Here is a simple example to connect to the MySQL server from the command prompt −

[root@host]# mysql -u root -p
Enter password:******

This will give you the mysql> command prompt where you will be able to execute any SQL command. Following is the result of above command −

The following code block shows the result of above code −

Welcome to the MySQL monitor. Commands end with ; or \g.
Your MySQL connection id is 2854760 to server version: 5.0.9

Type 'help;' or '\h' for help. Type '\c' to clear the buffer.

In the above example, we have used root as a user but you can use any other user as well. Any user will be able to perform all the SQL operations, which are allowed to that user.

You can disconnect from the MySQL database any time using the exitcommand at mysql> prompt.

mysql> exit
Bye

MySQL Connection Using PHP Script

PHP provides mysql_connect() function to open a database connection. This function takes five parameters and returns a MySQL link identifier on success or FALSE on failure.

Syntax

connection mysql_connect(server,user,passwd,new_link,client_flag);

S. No.	Parameter & Description
1	server Optional – The host name running the database server. If not specified, then the default value will be localhost:3306.
2	user Optional – The username accessing the database. If not specified, then the default will be the name of the user that owns the server process.
3	passwd Optional – The password of the user accessing the database. If not specified, then the default will be an empty password.

4	new_link	Optional – If a second call is made to mysql_connect() with the same arguments, no new connection will be established; instead, the identifier of the already opened connection will be returned.
5	client_flags	Optional – A combination of the following constants – • MYSQL_CLIENT_SSL – Use SSL encryption. • MYSQL_CLIENT_COMPRESS – Use compression protocol. • MYSQL_CLIENT_IGNORE_SPACE – Allow space after function names. • MYSQL_CLIENT_INTERACTIVE – Allow interactive timeout seconds of inactivity before closing the connection.

You can disconnect from the MySQL database anytime using another PHP function mysql_close(). This function takes a single parameter, which is a connection returned by the mysql_connect() function.

Syntax

bool mysql_close (resource $link_identifier);

If a resource is not specified, then the last opened database is closed. This function returns true if it closes the connection successfully otherwise it returns false.

Example

Try the following example to connect to a MySQL server −

```
<html>
  <head>
    <title>Connecting MySQL Server</title>
  </head>
  <body>
    <?php
      $dbhost = 'localhost:3306';
      $dbuser = 'guest';
      $dbpass = 'guest123';
      $conn = mysql_connect($dbhost, $dbuser, $dbpass);
      if(! $conn ) {
        die('Could not connect: ' . mysql_error());
      }
      echo 'Connected successfully';
      mysql_close($conn);
    ?>
  </body>
</html>
```

MySQL - Create Database

Create Database Using mysqladmin

You would need special privileges to create or to delete a MySQL database. So assuming you have access to the root user, you can create any database using the mysql mysqladmin binary.

Example

Here is a simple example to create a database called TUTORIALS −

[root@host]# mysqladmin -u root -p create TUTORIALS
Enter password:******

This will create a MySQL database called TUTORIALS.

Create a Database using PHP Script

PHP uses mysql_query function to create or delete a MySQL database. This function takes two parameters and returns TRUE on success or FALSE on failure.

Syntax

bool mysql_query(sql, connection);

S. No.	Parameter & Description
sql	Required - SQL query to create or delete a MySQL database
connection	Optional - if not specified, then the last opened connection by mysql_connect will be used.

Example

The following example to create a database −

```
<html>
   <head>
      <title>Creating MySQL Database</title>
   </head>
   <body>
      <?php
         $dbhost = 'localhost:3036';
         $dbuser = 'root';
         $dbpass = 'rootpassword';
         $conn = mysql_connect($dbhost, $dbuser, $dbpass);
         if(! $conn ) {
            die('Could not connect: ' . mysql_error());
         }
         echo 'Connected successfully<br />';
         $sql = 'CREATE DATABASE TUTORIALS';
         $retval = mysql_query( $sql, $conn );
```

```
   if(! $retval ) {
      die('Could not create database: ' . mysql_error());
   }
   echo "Database TUTORIALS created successfully\n";
   mysql_close($conn);
   ?>
 </body>
</html>
```

Drop MySQL Database

Drop a Database using mysqladmin

You would need special privileges to create or to delete a MySQL database. So, assuming you have access to the root user, you can create any database using the mysql mysqladmin binary.

Be careful while deleting any database because you will lose your all the data available in your database.

Here is an example to delete a database(TUTORIALS) created in the previous chapter –

[root@host]# mysqladmin -u root -p drop TUTORIALS
Enter password:******

This will give you a warning and it will confirm if you really want to delete this database or not.

Dropping the database is potentially a very bad thing to do.
Any data stored in the database will be destroyed.

Do you really want to drop the 'TUTORIALS' database [y/N] y
Database "TUTORIALS" dropped

Drop Database using PHP Script

PHP uses mysql_query function to create or delete a MySQL database. This function takes two parameters and returns TRUE on success or FALSE on failure.

Syntax

bool mysql_query(sql, connection);

Parameter	Description
sql	Required – SQL query to create or delete a MySQL database
connection	Optional – if not specified, then the last opened connection by mysql_connect will be used.

Example

Try the following example to delete a database –

```
<html>
  <head>
    <title>Deleting MySQL Database</title>
  </head>
  <body>
    <?php
      $dbhost = 'localhost:3036';
      $dbuser = 'root';
      $dbpass = 'rootpassword';
      $conn = mysql_connect($dbhost, $dbuser, $dbpass);
      if(! $conn ) {
        die('Could not connect: ' . mysql_error());
      }
      echo 'Connected successfully<br />';
      $sql = 'DROP DATABASE TUTORIALS';
```

```
   $retval = mysql_query( $sql, $conn );
   if(! $retval ) {
     die('Could not delete database: ' . mysql_error());
   }
   echo "Database TUTORIALS deleted successfully\n";
   mysql_close($conn);
  ?>
 </body>
</html>
```

WARNING – While deleting a database using the PHP script, it does not prompt you for any confirmation. So be careful while deleting a MySQL database.

Selecting MySQL Database

Once you get connected with the MySQL server, it is required to select a database to work with. This is because there might be more than one database available with the MySQL Server.

Selecting MySQL Database from the Command Prompt

It is very simple to select a database from the mysql> prompt. You can use the SQL command use to select a database.

Example

Here is an example to select a database called TUTORIALS −

```
[root@host]# mysql -u root -p
Enter password:******
mysql> use TUTORIALS;
Database changed
mysql>
```

Now, you have selected the TUTORIALS database and all the subsequent operations will be performed on the TUTORIALS database.

NOTE − All the database names, table names, table fields name are case sensitive. So you would have to use the proper names while giving any SQL command.

Selecting a MySQL Database Using PHP Script

PHP provides function mysql_select_db to select a database. It returns TRUE on success or FALSE on failure.

Syntax

bool mysql_select_db(db_name, connection);

S. No.	Parameter & Description
db_name	Required – MySQL Database name to be selected
connection	Optional – if not specified, then the last opened connection by mysql_connect will be used.

Example

Here is an example showing you how to select a database.

```
<html>
  <head>
    <title>Selecting MySQL Database</title>
  </head>
  <body>
    <?php
      $dbhost = 'localhost:3036';
      $dbuser = 'guest';
      $dbpass = 'guest123';
      $conn = mysql_connect($dbhost, $dbuser, $dbpass);
      if(! $conn ) {
        die('Could not connect: ' . mysql_error());
      }
      echo 'Connected successfully';
      mysql_select_db( 'TUTORIALS' );
      mysql_close($conn);
    ?>
  </body>
</html>
```

MySQL - Data Types

Properly defining the fields in a table is important to the overall optimization of your database. You should use only the type and size of field you really need to use. For example, do not define a field 10 characters wide, if you know you are only going to use 2 characters. These type of fields (or columns) are also referred to as data types, after the type of data you will be storing in those fields.

MySQL uses many different data types broken into three categories −
- Numeric
- Date and Time
- String Types.

Let us now discuss them in detail.

Numeric Data Types

MySQL uses all the standard ANSI SQL numeric data types, so if you're coming to MySQL from a different database system, these definitions will look familiar to you. The following list shows the common numeric data types and their descriptions −

- INT − A normal-sized integer that can be signed or unsigned. If signed, the allowable range is from -2147483648 to 2147483647. If unsigned, the allowable range is from 0 to 4294967295. You can specify a width of up to 11 digits.
- TINYINT − A very small integer that can be signed or unsigned. If signed, the allowable range is from -128 to 127. If unsigned, the allowable range is from 0 to 255. You can specify a width of up to 4 digits.
- SMALLINT − A small integer that can be signed or unsigned. If signed, the allowable range is from -32768 to 32767. If unsigned, the allowable range is from 0 to 65535. You can specify a width of up to 5 digits.

- MEDIUMINT – A medium-sized integer that can be signed or unsigned. If signed, the allowable range is from -8388608 to 8388607. If unsigned, the allowable range is from 0 to 16777215. You can specify a width of up to 9 digits.
- BIGINT – A large integer that can be signed or unsigned. If signed, the allowable range is from -9223372036854775808 to 9223372036854775807. If unsigned, the allowable range is from 0 to 18446744073709551615. You can specify a width of up to 20 digits.
- FLOAT(M,D) – A floating-point number that cannot be unsigned. You can define the display length (M) and the number of decimals (D). This is not required and will default to 10,2, where 2 is the number of decimals and 10 is the total number of digits (including decimals). Decimal precision can go to 24 places for a FLOAT.
- DOUBLE(M,D) – A double precision floating-point number that cannot be unsigned. You can define the display length (M) and the number of decimals (D). This is not required and will default to 16,4, where 4 is the number of decimals. Decimal precision can go to 53 places for a DOUBLE. REAL is a synonym for DOUBLE.
- DECIMAL(M,D) – An unpacked floating-point number that cannot be unsigned. In the unpacked decimals, each decimal corresponds to one byte. Defining the display length (M) and the number of decimals (D) is required. NUMERIC is a synonym for DECIMAL.

Date and Time Types

The MySQL date and time datatypes are as follows –

- DATE – A date in YYYY-MM-DD format, between 1000-01-01 and 9999-12-31. For example, December 30th, 1973 would be stored as 1973-12-30.
- DATETIME – A date and time combination in YYYY-MM-DD HH:MM:SS format, between 1000-01-01 00:00:00 and 9999-12-31 23:59:59. For example, 3:30 in the afternoon on December 30th, 1973 would be stored as 1973-12-30 15:30:00.
- TIMESTAMP – A timestamp between midnight, January 1st, 1970 and sometime in 2037. This looks like the previous DATETIME format, only

without the hyphens between numbers; 3:30 in the afternoon on December 30th, 1973 would be stored as 19731230153000 (YYYYMMDDHHMMSS).
- TIME – Stores the time in a HH:MM:SS format.
- YEAR(M) – Stores a year in a 2-digit or a 4-digit format. If the length is specified as 2 (for example YEAR(2)), YEAR can be between 1970 to 2069 (70 to 69). If the length is specified as 4, then YEAR can be 1901 to 2155. The default length is 4.

String Types

Although the numeric and date types are fun, most data you'll store will be in a string format. This list describes the common string datatypes in MySQL.

- CHAR(M) – A fixed-length string between 1 and 255 characters in length (for example CHAR(5)), right-padded with spaces to the specified length when stored. Defining a length is not required, but the default is 1.
- VARCHAR(M) – A variable-length string between 1 and 255 characters in length. For example, VARCHAR(25). You must define a length when creating a VARCHAR field.
- BLOB or TEXT – A field with a maximum length of 65535 characters. BLOBs are "Binary Large Objects" and are used to store large amounts of binary data, such as images or other types of files. Fields defined as TEXT also hold large amounts of data. The difference between the two is that the sorts and comparisons on the stored data are case sensitive on BLOBs and are not case sensitive in TEXT fields. You do not specify a length with BLOB or TEXT.
- TINYBLOB or TINYTEXT – A BLOB or TEXT column with a maximum length of 255 characters. You do not specify a length with TINYBLOB or TINYTEXT.
- MEDIUMBLOB or MEDIUMTEXT – A BLOB or TEXT column with a maximum length of 16777215 characters. You do not specify a length with MEDIUMBLOB or MEDIUMTEXT.
- LONGBLOB or LONGTEXT – A BLOB or TEXT column with a maximum length of 4294967295 characters. You do not specify a length with LONGBLOB or LONGTEXT.

- ENUM – An enumeration, which is a fancy term for list. When defining an ENUM, you are creating a list of items from which the value must be selected (or it can be NULL). For example, if you wanted your field to contain "A" or "B" or "C", you would define your ENUM as ENUM ('A', 'B', 'C') and only those values (or NULL) could ever populate that field.

In the next chapter, we will discuss how to create tables in MySQL.

Create MySQL Tables

To begin with, the table creation command requires the following details –

- Name of the table
- Name of the fields
- Definitions for each field

Syntax

Here is a generic SQL syntax to create a MySQL table –

CREATE TABLE table_name (column_name column_type);

Now, we will create the following table in the TUTORIALS database.

```
create table tutorials_tbl(
   tutorial_id INT NOT NULL AUTO_INCREMENT,
   tutorial_title VARCHAR(100) NOT NULL,
   tutorial_author VARCHAR(40) NOT NULL,
   submission_date DATE,
   PRIMARY KEY ( tutorial_id )
);
```

Here, a few items need explanation –

- Field Attribute NOT NULL is being used because we do not want this field to be NULL. So, if a user will try to create a record with a NULL value, then MySQL will raise an error.
- Field Attribute AUTO_INCREMENT tells MySQL to go ahead and add the next available number to the id field.
- Keyword PRIMARY KEY is used to define a column as a primary key. You can use multiple columns separated by a comma to define a primary key.

Creating Tables from Command Prompt

It is easy to create a MySQL table from the mysql> prompt. You will use the SQL command CREATE TABLE to create a table.

Example

Here is an example, which will create tutorials_tbl −

root@host# mysql -u root -p
Enter password:*******
mysql> use TUTORIALS;
Database changed
mysql> CREATE TABLE tutorials_tbl(
  -> tutorial_id INT NOT NULL AUTO_INCREMENT,
  -> tutorial_title VARCHAR(100) NOT NULL,
  -> tutorial_author VARCHAR(40) NOT NULL,
  -> submission_date DATE,
  -> PRIMARY KEY (tutorial_id)
  ->);
Query OK, 0 rows affected (0.16 sec)
mysql>

NOTE − MySQL does not terminate a command until you give a semicolon (;) at the end of SQL command.

Creating Tables Using PHP Script

To create new table in any existing database you would need to use PHP function mysql_query(). You will pass its second argument with a proper SQL command to create a table.

Example

The following program is an example to create a table using PHP script –

```php
<html>
 <head>
  <title>Creating MySQL Tables</title>
 </head>
 <body>
  <?php
   $dbhost = 'localhost:3036';
   $dbuser = 'root';
   $dbpass = 'rootpassword';
   $conn = mysql_connect($dbhost, $dbuser, $dbpass);
   if(! $conn ) {
      die('Could not connect: ' . mysql_error());
   }
   echo 'Connected successfully<br />';
   $sql = "CREATE TABLE tutorials_tbl( ".
      "tutorial_id INT NOT NULL AUTO_INCREMENT, ".
      "tutorial_title VARCHAR(100) NOT NULL, ".
      "tutorial_author VARCHAR(40) NOT NULL, ".
      "submission_date DATE, ".
      "PRIMARY KEY ( tutorial_id )); ";
   mysql_select_db( 'TUTORIALS' );
   $retval = mysql_query( $sql, $conn );
   if(! $retval ) {
      die('Could not create table: ' . mysql_error());
   }
   echo "Table created successfully\n";
   mysql_close($conn);
  ?>
 </body>
</html>
```

Drop MySQL Tables

It is very easy to drop an existing MySQL table, but you need to be very careful while deleting any existing table because the data lost will not be recovered after deleting a table.

Syntax

Here is a generic SQL syntax to drop a MySQL table –

DROP TABLE table_name ;

Dropping Tables from the Command Prompt

To drop tables from the command prompt, we need to execute the DROP TABLE SQL command at the mysql> prompt.

Example

The following program is an example which deletes the tutorials_tbl –

```
root@host# mysql -u root -p
Enter password:*******
mysql> use TUTORIALS;
Database changed
mysql> DROP TABLE tutorials_tbl
Query OK, 0 rows affected (0.8 sec)
mysql>
```

Dropping Tables Using PHP Script

To drop an existing table in any database, you would need to use the PHP function mysql_query(). You will pass its second argument with a proper SQL command to drop a table.

Example

```
<html>
 <head>
   <title>Creating MySQL Tables</title>
 </head>
 <body>
   <?php
     $dbhost = 'localhost:3036';
     $dbuser = 'root';
     $dbpass = 'rootpassword';
     $conn = mysql_connect($dbhost, $dbuser, $dbpass);
     if(! $conn ) {
        die('Could not connect: ' . mysql_error());
     }
     echo 'Connected successfully<br />';
     $sql = "DROP TABLE tutorials_tbl";
     mysql_select_db( 'TUTORIALS' );
     $retval = mysql_query( $sql, $conn );
     if(! $retval ) {
        die('Could not delete table: ' . mysql_error());
     }
     echo "Table deleted successfully\n";
     mysql_close($conn);
   ?>
 </body>
</html>
```

MySQL - Insert Query

To insert data into a MySQL table, you would need to use the SQL INSERT INTO command. You can insert data into the MySQL table by using the mysql> prompt or by using any script like PHP.

Syntax

Here is a generic SQL syntax of INSERT INTO command to insert data into the MySQL table −

```
INSERT INTO table_name ( field1, field2,...fieldN )
   VALUES
   ( value1, value2,...valueN );
```

To insert string data types, it is required to keep all the values into double or single quotes. For example "value".

Inserting Data from the Command Prompt

To insert data from the command prompt, we will use SQL INSERT INTO command to insert data into MySQL table tutorials_tbl.

Example

The following example will create 3 records into tutorials_tbl table –

```
root@host# mysql -u root -p password;
Enter password:******
mysql> use TUTORIALS;
Database changed

mysql> INSERT INTO tutorials_tbl
  ->(tutorial_title, tutorial_author, submission_date)
  ->VALUES
  ->("Learn PHP", "John Poul", NOW());
Query OK, 1 row affected (0.01 sec)

mysql> INSERT INTO tutorials_tbl
  ->(tutorial_title, tutorial_author, submission_date)
  ->VALUES
  ->("Learn MySQL", "Abdul S", NOW());
Query OK, 1 row affected (0.01 sec)

mysql> INSERT INTO tutorials_tbl
  ->(tutorial_title, tutorial_author, submission_date)
  ->VALUES
  ->("JAVA Tutorial", "Sanjay", '2007-05-06');
Query OK, 1 row affected (0.01 sec)
mysql>
```

NOTE – Please note that all the arrow signs (->) are not a part of the SQL command. They are indicating a new line and they are created automatically by the MySQL prompt while pressing the enter key without giving a semicolon at the end of each line of the command.

In the above example, we have not provided a tutorial_id because at the time of table creation, we had given AUTO_INCREMENT option for this field. So MySQL takes care of inserting these IDs automatically. Here, NOW() is a MySQL function, which returns the current date and time.

Inserting Data Using a PHP Script

You can use the same SQL INSERT INTO command into the PHP function mysql_query() to insert data into a MySQL table.

Example

This example will take three parameters from the user and will insert them into the MySQL table –

```
<html>
  <head>
    <title>Add New Record in MySQL Database</title>
  </head>

  <body>
    <?php
      if(isset($_POST['add'])) {
        $dbhost = 'localhost:3036';
        $dbuser = 'root';
        $dbpass = 'rootpassword';
        $conn = mysql_connect($dbhost, $dbuser, $dbpass);

        if(! $conn ) {
          die('Could not connect: ' . mysql_error());
        }

        if(! get_magic_quotes_gpc() ) {
          $tutorial_title = addslashes ($_POST['tutorial_title']);
          $tutorial_author = addslashes ($_POST['tutorial_author']);
        } else {
          $tutorial_title = $_POST['tutorial_title'];
          $tutorial_author = $_POST['tutorial_author'];
        }
```

```php
    $submission_date = $_POST['submission_date'];

    $sql = "INSERT INTO tutorials_tbl ".
        "(tutorial_title,tutorial_author, submission_date) "."VALUES ".
        "('$tutorial_title','$tutorial_author','$submission_date')";
        mysql_select_db('TUTORIALS');
    $retval = mysql_query( $sql, $conn );

    if(! $retval ) {
        die('Could not enter data: ' . mysql_error());
    }

    echo "Entered data successfully\n";
    mysql_close($conn);
  } else {
?>

<form method = "post" action = "<?php $_PHP_SELF ?>">
  <table width = "600" border = "0" cellspacing = "1" cellpadding = "2">
    <tr>
      <td width = "250">Tutorial Title</td>
      <td>
        <input name = "tutorial_title" type = "text" id = "tutorial_title">
      </td>
    </tr>

    <tr>
      <td width = "250">Tutorial Author</td>
      <td>
        <input name = "tutorial_author" type = "text" id = "tutorial_author">
      </td>
    </tr>

    <tr>
      <td width = "250">Submission Date [ yyyy-mm-dd ]</td>
      <td>
        <input name = "submission_date" type = "text" id = "submission_date">
```

```
        </td>
      </tr>

      <tr>
        <td width = "250"> </td>
        <td> </td>
      </tr>

      <tr>
        <td width = "250"> </td>
        <td>
          <input name = "add" type = "submit" id = "add"  value = "Add Tutorial">
        </td>
      </tr>
    </table>
  </form>
 <?php
   }
 ?>
 </body>
</html>
```

While doing a data insert, it is best to use the function get_magic_quotes_gpc() to check if the current configuration for magic quote is set or not. If this function returns false, then use the function addslashes() to add slashes before the quotes.

You can put many validations around to check if the entered data is correct or not and can take the appropriate action.

MySQL - Select Query

The SQL SELECT command is used to fetch data from the MySQL database. You can use this command at mysql> prompt as well as in any script like PHP.

Syntax

Here is generic SQL syntax of SELECT command to fetch data from the MySQL table −

SELECT field1, field2,...fieldN
FROM table_name1, table_name2...
[WHERE Clause]
[OFFSET M][LIMIT N]

- You can use one or more tables separated by comma to include various conditions using a WHERE clause, but the WHERE clause is an optional part of the SELECT command.
- You can fetch one or more fields in a single SELECT command.
- You can specify star (*) in place of fields. In this case, SELECT will return all the fields.
- You can specify any condition using the WHERE clause.
- You can specify an offset using OFFSET from where SELECT will start returning records. By default, the offset starts at zero.
- You can limit the number of returns using the LIMIT attribute.

Fetching Data from a Command Prompt

This will use SQL SELECT command to fetch data from the MySQL table tutorials_tbl.

Example

The following example will return all the records from the tutorials_tbl table −

```
root@host# mysql -u root -p password;
Enter password:*******
mysql> use TUTORIALS;
Database changed
mysql> SELECT * from tutorials_tbl
+-------------+-----------------+-----------------+-----------------+
| tutorial_id | tutorial_title | tutorial_author | submission_date |
+-------------+-----------------+-----------------+-----------------+
|      1 | Learn PHP      | John Poul  | 2007-05-21 |
|      2 | Learn MySQL    | Abdul S    | 2007-05-21 |
|      3 | JAVA Tutorial  | Sanjay     | 2007-05-21 |
+-------------+-----------------+-----------------+-----------------+
3 rows in set (0.01 sec)

mysql>
```

Fetching Data Using a PHP Script

You can use the same SQL SELECT command into a PHP function mysql_query(). This function is used to execute the SQL command and then later another PHP function mysql_fetch_array() can be used to fetch all the selected data. This function returns the row as an associative array, a numeric array, or both. This function returns FALSE if there are no more rows.

The following program is a simple example which will show how to fetch / display records from the tutorials_tbl table.

Example

The following code block will display all the records from the tutorials_tbl table.

```php
<?php
$dbhost = 'localhost:3036';
$dbuser = 'root';
$dbpass = 'rootpassword';
$conn = mysql_connect($dbhost, $dbuser, $dbpass);

if(! $conn ) {
   die('Could not connect: ' . mysql_error());
}
$sql = 'SELECT tutorial_id, tutorial_title, tutorial_author, submission_date
   FROM tutorials_tbl';

mysql_select_db('TUTORIALS');
$retval = mysql_query( $sql, $conn );

if(! $retval ) {
   die('Could not get data: ' . mysql_error());
}

while($row = mysql_fetch_array($retval, MYSQL_ASSOC)) {
   echo "Tutorial ID :{$row['tutorial_id']} <br> ".
      "Title: {$row['tutorial_title']} <br> ".
      "Author: {$row['tutorial_author']} <br> ".
      "Submission Date : {$row['submission_date']} <br> ".
      "--------------------------------<br>";
}
echo "Fetched data successfully\n";
mysql_close($conn);
?>
```

The content of the rows is assigned to the variable $row and the values in that row are then printed.

NOTE – Always remember to put curly brackets when you want to insert an array value directly into a string.

In the above example, the constant MYSQL_ASSOC is used as the second argument to the PHP function mysql_fetch_array(), so that it returns the row as an associative array. With an associative array you can access the field by using their name instead of using the index.

PHP provides another function called mysql_fetch_assoc(), which also returns the row as an associative array.

Example

The following example to display all the records from the tutorial_tbl table using mysql_fetch_assoc() function.

```php
<?php
  $dbhost = 'localhost:3036';
  $dbuser = 'root';
  $dbpass = 'rootpassword';
  $conn = mysql_connect($dbhost, $dbuser, $dbpass);

  if(! $conn ) {
    die('Could not connect: ' . mysql_error());
  }

  $sql = 'SELECT tutorial_id, tutorial_title, tutorial_author, submission_date
    FROM tutorials_tbl';

  mysql_select_db('TUTORIALS');
  $retval = mysql_query( $sql, $conn );

  if(! $retval ) {
    die('Could not get data: ' . mysql_error());
  }
```

```
  while($row = mysql_fetch_assoc($retval)) {
    echo "Tutorial ID :{$row['tutorial_id']} <br> ".
      "Title: {$row['tutorial_title']} <br> ".
      "Author: {$row['tutorial_author']} <br> ".
      "Submission Date : {$row['submission_date']} <br> ".
      "--------------------------------<br>";
  }
  echo "Fetched data successfully\n";
  mysql_close($conn);
?>
```

You can also use the constant MYSQL_NUM as the second argument to the PHP function mysql_fetch_array(). This will cause the function to return an array with the numeric index.

Example

Try out the following example to display all the records from tutorials_tbl table using the MYSQL_NUM argument.

```
<?php
  $dbhost = 'localhost:3036';
  $dbuser = 'root';
  $dbpass = 'rootpassword';
  $conn = mysql_connect($dbhost, $dbuser, $dbpass);

  if(! $conn ) {
    die('Could not connect: ' . mysql_error());
  }

  $sql = 'SELECT tutorial_id, tutorial_title, tutorial_author, submission_date
    FROM tutorials_tbl';

  mysql_select_db('TUTORIALS');
  $retval = mysql_query( $sql, $conn );
```

```php
if(! $retval ) {
    die('Could not get data: ' . mysql_error());
}

while($row = mysql_fetch_array($retval, MYSQL_NUM)) {
    echo "Tutorial ID :{$row[0]}  <br> ".
      "Title: {$row[1]} <br> ".
      "Author: {$row[2]} <br> ".
      "Submission Date : {$row[3]} <br> ".
      "--------------------------------<br>";
}
echo "Fetched data successfully\n";
mysql_close($conn);
?>
```

All the above three examples will produce the same result.

Releasing Memory

It is a good practice to release cursor memory at the end of each SELECT statement. This can be done by using the PHP function mysql_free_result(). The following program is the example to show how it should be used.

Example

Try out the following example −

```php
<?php
   $dbhost = 'localhost:3036';
   $dbuser = 'root';
   $dbpass = 'rootpassword';
   $conn = mysql_connect($dbhost, $dbuser, $dbpass);
   
   if(! $conn ) {
      die('Could not connect: ' . mysql_error());
   }
   
   $sql = 'SELECT tutorial_id, tutorial_title, tutorial_author, submission_date
      FROM tutorials_tbl';
   
   mysql_select_db('TUTORIALS');
   $retval = mysql_query( $sql, $conn );
   
   if(! $retval ) {
      die('Could not get data: ' . mysql_error());
   }
   
   while($row = mysql_fetch_array($retval, MYSQL_NUM)) {
      echo "Tutorial ID :{$row[0]}  <br> ".
         "Title: {$row[1]} <br> ".
         "Author: {$row[2]} <br> ".
         "Submission Date : {$row[3]} <br> ".
         "--------------------------------<br>";
   }
   mysql_free_result($retval);
   echo "Fetched data successfully\n";
   mysql_close($conn);
?>
```

While fetching data, you can write as complex a code as you like, but the procedure will remain the same as mentioned above.

MySQL - WHERE Clause

We have seen the SQL SELECT command to fetch data from a MySQL table. We can use a conditional clause called the WHERE Clause to filter out the results. Using this WHERE clause, we can specify a selection criteria to select the required records from a table.

Syntax

The following code block has a generic SQL syntax of the SELECT command with the WHERE clause to fetch data from the MySQL table −

SELECT field1, field2,...fieldN table_name1, table_name2...
[WHERE condition1 [AND [OR]] condition2.....

- You can use one or more tables separated by a comma to include various conditions using a WHERE clause, but the WHERE clause is an optional part of the SELECT command.
- You can specify any condition using the WHERE clause.
- You can specify more than one condition using the AND or the ORoperators.
- A WHERE clause can be used along with DELETE or UPDATE SQL command also to specify a condition.

The WHERE clause works like an if condition in any programming language. This clause is used to compare the given value with the field value available in a MySQL table. If the given value from outside is equal to the available field value in the MySQL table, then it returns that row.

Here is the list of operators, which can be used with the WHERE clause.

Assume field A holds 10 and field B holds 20, then −

Operator	Description	Example
=	Checks if the values of the two operands are equal or not, if yes, then the condition becomes true.	(A = B) is not true.
!=	Checks if the values of the two operands are equal or not, if the values are not equal then the condition becomes true.	(A != B) is true.
>	Checks if the value of the left operand is greater than the value of the right operand, if yes, then the condition becomes true.	(A > B) is not true.
<	Checks if the value of the left operand is less than the value of the right operand, if yes then the condition becomes true.	(A < B) is true.
>=	Checks if the value of the left operand is greater than or equal to the value of the right operand, if yes, then the condition becomes true.	(A >= B) is not true.
<=	Checks if the value of the left operand is less than or equal to the value of the right operand, if yes, then the condition becomes true.	(A <= B) is true.

The WHERE clause is very useful when you want to fetch the selected rows from a table, especially when you use the MySQL Join. Joins are discussed in another chapter.

It is a common practice to search for records using the Primary Key to make the search faster.

If the given condition does not match any record in the table, then the query would not return any row.

Fetching Data from the Command Prompt

This will use the SQL SELECT command with the WHERE clause to fetch the selected data from the MySQL table – tutorials_tbl.

Example

The following example will return all the records from the tutorials_tbl table for which the author name is Sanjay.

```
root@host# mysql -u root -p password;
Enter password:*******
mysql> use TUTORIALS;
Database changed
mysql> SELECT * from tutorials_tbl WHERE tutorial_author = 'Sanjay';
+-------------+----------------+-----------------+-----------------+
| tutorial_id | tutorial_title | tutorial_author | submission_date |
+-------------+----------------+-----------------+-----------------+
|      3      | JAVA Tutorial  |     Sanjay      |   2007-05-21    |
+-------------+----------------+-----------------+-----------------+
1 rows in set (0.01 sec)

mysql>
```

Unless performing a LIKE comparison on a string, the comparison is not case sensitive. You can make your search case sensitive by using the BINARYkeyword as follows −

root@host# mysql -u root -p password;
Enter password:*******
mysql> use TUTORIALS;
Database changed
mysql> SELECT * from tutorials_tbl \
   WHERE BINARY tutorial_author = 'sanjay';
Empty set (0.02 sec)

mysql>

Fetching Data Using a PHP Script

You can use the same SQL SELECT command with the WHERE CLAUSE into the PHP function mysql_query(). This function is used to execute the SQL command and later another PHP function mysql_fetch_array() can be used to fetch all the selected data. This function returns a row as an associative array, a numeric array, or both. This function returns FALSE if there are no more rows.

Example

The following example will return all the records from the tutorials_tbl table for which the author name is Sanjay −

```php
<?php
   $dbhost = 'localhost:3036';
   $dbuser = 'root';
   $dbpass = 'rootpassword';
   $conn = mysql_connect($dbhost, $dbuser, $dbpass);
   
   if(! $conn ) {
      die('Could not connect: ' . mysql_error());
   }
   
   $sql = 'SELECT tutorial_id, tutorial_title,
            tutorial_author, submission_date
            FROM tutorials_tbl
            WHERE tutorial_author = "Sanjay"';
   
   mysql_select_db('TUTORIALS');
   $retval = mysql_query( $sql, $conn );
   
   if(! $retval ) {
      die('Could not get data: ' . mysql_error());
   }
   
   while($row = mysql_fetch_array($retval, MYSQL_ASSOC)) {
      echo "Tutorial ID :{$row['tutorial_id']}  <br> ".
         "Title: {$row['tutorial_title']} <br> ".
         "Author: {$row['tutorial_author']} <br> ".
         "Submission Date : {$row['submission_date']} <br> ".
         "--------------------------------<br>";
   }
   echo "Fetched data successfully\n";
   mysql_close($conn);
?>
```

MySQL - UPDATE Query

There may be a requirement where the existing data in a MySQL table needs to be modified. You can do so by using the SQL UPDATE command. This will modify any field value of any MySQL table.

Syntax

The following code block has a generic SQL syntax of the UPDATE command to modify the data in the MySQL table −

```
UPDATE table_name SET field1 = new-value1, field2 = new-value2
[WHERE Clause]
```

- You can update one or more field altogether.
- You can specify any condition using the WHERE clause.
- You can update the values in a single table at a time.

The WHERE clause is very useful when you want to update the selected rows in a table.

Updating Data from the Command Prompt

This will use the SQL UPDATE command with the WHERE clause to update the selected data in the MySQL table tutorials_tbl.

Example

The following example will update the tutorial_title field for a record having the tutorial_id as 3.

```
root@host# mysql -u root -p password;
Enter password:*******

mysql> use TUTORIALS;
Database changed

mysql> UPDATE tutorials_tbl
   -> SET tutorial_title = 'Learning JAVA'
   -> WHERE tutorial_id = 3;
Query OK, 1 row affected (0.04 sec)
Rows matched: 1  Changed: 1  Warnings: 0

mysql>
```

Updating Data Using a PHP Script

You can use the SQL UPDATE command with or without the WHERE CLAUSE into the PHP function – mysql_query(). This function will execute the SQL command in a similar way it is executed at the mysql> prompt.

Example

The following example to update the tutorial_title field for a record having tutorial_id as 3.

```php
<?php
   $dbhost = 'localhost:3036';
   $dbuser = 'root';
   $dbpass = 'rootpassword';
   $conn = mysql_connect($dbhost, $dbuser, $dbpass);
   
   if(! $conn ) {
      die('Could not connect: ' . mysql_error());
   }
   
   $sql = 'UPDATE tutorials_tbl
      SET tutorial_title="Learning JAVA"
      WHERE tutorial_id=3';
   
   mysql_select_db('TUTORIALS');
   $retval = mysql_query( $sql, $conn );
   
   if(! $retval ) {
      die('Could not update data: ' . mysql_error());
   }
   echo "Updated data successfully\n";
   mysql_close($conn);
?>
```

MySQL - DELETE Query

If you want to delete a record from any MySQL table, then you can use the SQL command DELETE FROM. You can use this command at the mysql> prompt as well as in any script like PHP.

Syntax

The following code block has a generic SQL syntax of the DELETE command to delete data from a MySQL table.

DELETE FROM table_name [WHERE Clause]

- If the WHERE clause is not specified, then all the records will be deleted from the given MySQL table.
- You can specify any condition using the WHERE clause.
- You can delete records in a single table at a time.

The WHERE clause is very useful when you want to delete selected rows in a table.

Deleting Data from the Command Prompt

This will use the SQL DELETE command with the WHERE clause to delete selected data into the MySQL table – tutorials_tbl.

Example

The following example will delete a record from the tutorial_tbl whose tutorial_id is 3.

root@host# mysql -u root -p password;
Enter password:*******

mysql> use TUTORIALS;
Database changed

mysql> DELETE FROM tutorials_tbl WHERE tutorial_id=3;
Query OK, 1 row affected (0.23 sec)

mysql>

Deleting Data Using a PHP Script

You can use the SQL DELETE command with or without the WHERE CLAUSE into the PHP function – mysql_query(). This function will execute the SQL command in the same way as it is executed at the mysql> prompt.

Example

Try the following example to delete a record from the tutorial_tbl whose tutorial_id is 3.

```php
<?php
   $dbhost = 'localhost:3036';
   $dbuser = 'root';
   $dbpass = 'rootpassword';
   $conn = mysql_connect($dbhost, $dbuser, $dbpass);

   if(! $conn ) {
      die('Could not connect: ' . mysql_error());
   }

   $sql = 'DELETE FROM tutorials_tbl
      WHERE tutorial_id=3';

   mysql_select_db('TUTORIALS');
   $retval = mysql_query( $sql, $conn );

   if(! $retval ) {
      die('Could not delete data: ' . mysql_error());
   }
   echo "Deleted data successfully\n";
   mysql_close($conn);
?>
```

MySQL - LIKE Clause

We have seen the SQL SELECT command to fetch data from the MySQL table. We can also use a conditional clause called as the WHERE clause to select the required records.

A WHERE clause with the 'equal to' sign (=) works fine where we want to do an exact match. Like if "tutorial_author = 'Sanjay'". But there may be a requirement where we want to filter out all the results where tutorial_author name should contain "jay". This can be handled using SQL LIKE Clause along with the WHERE clause.

If the SQL LIKE clause is used along with the % character, then it will work like a meta character (*) as in UNIX, while listing out all the files or directories at the command prompt. Without a % character, the LIKE clause is very same as the equal to sign along with the WHERE clause.

Syntax

The following code block has a generic SQL syntax of the SELECT command along with the LIKE clause to fetch data from a MySQL table.

SELECT field1, field2,...fieldN table_name1, table_name2...
WHERE field1 LIKE condition1 [AND [OR]] filed2 = 'somevalue'

- You can specify any condition using the WHERE clause.
- You can use the LIKE clause along with the WHERE clause.
- You can use the LIKE clause in place of the equals to sign.
- When LIKE is used along with % sign then it will work like a meta character search.
- You can specify more than one condition using AND or OR operators.
- A WHERE...LIKE clause can be used along with DELETE or UPDATE SQL command also to specify a condition.

Using the LIKE clause at the Command Prompt

This will use the SQL SELECT command with the WHERE...LIKE clause to fetch the selected data from the MySQL table – tutorials_tbl.

Example

The following example will return all the records from the tutorials_tbl table for which the author name ends with jay –

```
root@host# mysql -u root -p password;
Enter password:*******
mysql> use TUTORIALS;
Database changed
mysql> SELECT * from tutorials_tbl
   -> WHERE tutorial_author LIKE '%jay';
+-------------+-----------------+-----------------+-----------------+
| tutorial_id | tutorial_title  | tutorial_author | submission_date |
+-------------+-----------------+-----------------+-----------------+
|     3       | JAVA Tutorial   | Sanjay          | 2007-05-21      |
+-------------+-----------------+-----------------+-----------------+
1 rows in set (0.01 sec)

mysql>
```

Using LIKE clause inside PHP Script

You can use similar syntax of the WHERE...LIKE clause into the PHP function – mysql_query(). This function is used to execute the SQL command and later another PHP function – mysql_fetch_array() can be used to fetch all the selected data, if the WHERE...LIKE clause is used along with the SELECT command.

But if the WHERE...LIKE clause is being used with the DELETE or UPDATE command, then no further PHP function call is required.

Example

Try out the following example to return all the records from the tutorials_tbl table for which the author name contains jay –

```php
<?php
   $dbhost = 'localhost:3036';
   $dbuser = 'root';
   $dbpass = 'rootpassword';
   $conn = mysql_connect($dbhost, $dbuser, $dbpass);
   
   if(! $conn ) {
      die('Could not connect: ' . mysql_error());
   }
   $sql = 'SELECT tutorial_id, tutorial_title,
      tutorial_author, submission_date
      FROM tutorials_tbl
      WHERE tutorial_author LIKE "%jay%"';
   
   mysql_select_db('TUTORIALS');
   $retval = mysql_query( $sql, $conn );
   
   if(! $retval ) {
      die('Could not get data: ' . mysql_error());
   }
   
   while($row = mysql_fetch_array($retval, MYSQL_ASSOC)) {
      echo "Tutorial ID :{$row['tutorial_id']}  <br> ".
         "Title: {$row['tutorial_title']} <br> ".
         "Author: {$row['tutorial_author']} <br> ".
         "Submission Date : {$row['submission_date']} <br> ".
         "--------------------------------<br>";
   }
   echo "Fetched data successfully\n";
   mysql_close($conn);
?>
```

MySQL - Sorting Results

We have seen the SQL SELECT command to fetch data from a MySQL table. When you select rows, the MySQL server is free to return them in any order, unless you instruct it otherwise by saying how to sort the result. But, you sort a result set by adding an ORDER BY clause that names the column or columns which you want to sort.

Syntax

The following code block is a generic SQL syntax of the SELECT command along with the ORDER BY clause to sort the data from a MySQL table.

```
SELECT field1, field2,...fieldN table_name1, table_name2...
ORDER BY field1, [field2...] [ASC [DESC]]
```

- You can sort the returned result on any field, if that field is being listed out.
- You can sort the result on more than one field.
- You can use the keyword ASC or DESC to get result in ascending or descending order. By default, it's the ascending order.
- You can use the WHERE...LIKE clause in the usual way to put a condition.

Using ORDER BY clause at the Command Prompt

This will use the SQL SELECT command with the ORDER BY clause to fetch data from the MySQL table – tutorials_tbl.

Example

Try out the following example, which returns the result in an ascending order.

```
root@host# mysql -u root -p password;
Enter password:*******
mysql> use TUTORIALS;
Database changed
mysql> SELECT * from tutorials_tbl ORDER BY tutorial_author ASC
+-------------+----------------+-----------------+-----------------+
| tutorial_id | tutorial_title | tutorial_author | submission_date |
+-------------+----------------+-----------------+-----------------+
|     2       | Learn MySQL    |    Abdul S      |   2007-05-24    |
|     1       | Learn PHP      |    John Poul    |   2007-05-24    |
|     3       | JAVA Tutorial  |    Sanjay       |   2007-05-06    |
+-------------+----------------+-----------------+-----------------+
3 rows in set (0.42 sec)

mysql>
```

Verify all the author names that are listed out in the ascending order.

Using ORDER BY clause inside a PHP Script

You can use a similar syntax of the ORDER BY clause into the PHP function – mysql_query(). This function is used to execute the SQL command and later another PHP function mysql_fetch_array() can be used to fetch all the selected data.

Example

Try out the following example, which returns the result in a descending order of the tutorial authors.

```php
<?php
   $dbhost = 'localhost:3036';
   $dbuser = 'root';
   $dbpass = 'rootpassword';
   $conn = mysql_connect($dbhost, $dbuser, $dbpass);

   if(! $conn ) {
      die('Could not connect: ' . mysql_error());
   }
   $sql = 'SELECT tutorial_id, tutorial_title,
      tutorial_author, submission_date
      FROM tutorials_tbl
      ORDER BY  tutorial_author DESC';

   mysql_select_db('TUTORIALS');
   $retval = mysql_query( $sql, $conn );

   if(! $retval ) {
      die('Could not get data: ' . mysql_error());
   }

   while($row = mysql_fetch_array($retval, MYSQL_ASSOC)) {
      echo "Tutorial ID :{$row['tutorial_id']}  <br> ".
      "Title: {$row['tutorial_title']} <br> ".
      "Author: {$row['tutorial_author']} <br> ".
      "Submission Date : {$row['submission_date']} <br> ".
      "--------------------------------<br>";
   }
   echo "Fetched data successfully\n";
   mysql_close($conn);
?>
```

Using MySQl Joins

In the previous chapters, we were getting data from one table at a time. This is good enough for simple takes, but in most of the real world MySQL usages, you will often need to get data from multiple tables in a single query.

You can use multiple tables in your single SQL query. The act of joining in MySQL refers to smashing two or more tables into a single table.

You can use JOINS in the SELECT, UPDATE and DELETE statements to join the MySQL tables. We will see an example of the LEFT JOIN also which is different from the simple MySQL JOIN.

Using Joins at the Command Prompt

Assume we have two tables tcount_tbl and tutorials_tbl, in TUTORIALS. Now take a look at the examples given below –

Example

The following examples –

```
root@host# mysql -u root -p password;
Enter password:******
mysql> use TUTORIALS;
Database changed
mysql> SELECT * FROM tcount_tbl;
+-----------------+----------------+
| tutorial_author | tutorial_count |
+-----------------+----------------+
|     mahran      |      20        |
|     mahnaz      |     NULL       |
|      Jen        |     NULL       |
|      Gill       |      20        |
```

| John Poul | 1 |
| Sanjay | 1 |
+-----------------+----------------+
6 rows in set (0.01 sec)
mysql> SELECT * from tutorials_tbl;
+-------------+----------------+----------------+----------------+
| tutorial_id | tutorial_title | tutorial_author | submission_date |
+-------------+----------------+----------------+----------------+
1	Learn PHP	John Poul	2007-05-24
2	Learn MySQL	Abdul S	2007-05-24
3	JAVA Tutorial	Sanjay	2007-05-06
+-------------+----------------+----------------+----------------+
3 rows in set (0.00 sec)
mysql>

Now we can write an SQL query to join these two tables. This query will select all the authors from table tutorials_tbl and will pick up the corresponding number of tutorials from the tcount_tbl.

mysql> SELECT a.tutorial_id, a.tutorial_author, b.tutorial_count
   -> FROM tutorials_tbl a, tcount_tbl b
   -> WHERE a.tutorial_author = b.tutorial_author;
+-------------+----------------+----------------+
| tutorial_id | tutorial_author | tutorial_count |
+-------------+----------------+----------------+
| 1 | John Poul | 1 |
| 3 | Sanjay | 1 |
+-------------+----------------+----------------+
2 rows in set (0.01 sec)
mysql>

Using Joins in a PHP Script

You can use any of the above-mentioned SQL query in the PHP script. You only need to pass the SQL query into the PHP function mysql_query() and then you will fetch results in the usual way.

Example

The following example –

```php
<?php
   $dbhost = 'localhost:3036';
   $dbuser = 'root';
   $dbpass = 'rootpassword';
   $conn = mysql_connect($dbhost, $dbuser, $dbpass);
   
   if(! $conn ) {
      die('Could not connect: ' . mysql_error());
   }
   
   $sql = 'SELECT a.tutorial_id, a.tutorial_author, b.tutorial_count
      FROM tutorials_tbl a, tcount_tbl b
      WHERE a.tutorial_author = b.tutorial_author';
   
   mysql_select_db('TUTORIALS');
   $retval = mysql_query( $sql, $conn );
   
   if(! $retval ) {
      die('Could not get data: ' . mysql_error());
   }
   
   while($row = mysql_fetch_array($retval, MYSQL_ASSOC)) {
      echo "Author:{$row['tutorial_author']} <br> ".
      "Count: {$row['tutorial_count']} <br> ".
      "Tutorial ID: {$row['tutorial_id']} <br> ".
      "--------------------------------<br>";
   }
   echo "Fetched data successfully\n";
   mysql_close($conn);
?>
```

MySQL LEFT JOIN

A MySQL left join is different from a simple join. A MySQL LEFT JOIN gives some extra consideration to the table that is on the left.

If I do a LEFT JOIN, I get all the records that match in the same way and IN ADDITION I get an extra record for each unmatched record in the left table of the join: thus ensuring (in my example) that every AUTHOR gets a mention.

Example

Try the following example to understand the LEFT JOIN.

```
root@host# mysql -u root -p password;
Enter password:*******
mysql> use TUTORIALS;
Database changed
mysql> SELECT a.tutorial_id, a.tutorial_author, b.tutorial_count
   -> FROM tutorials_tbl a LEFT JOIN tcount_tbl b
   -> ON a.tutorial_author = b.tutorial_author;
+-------------+-----------------+---------------+
| tutorial_id | tutorial_author | tutorial_count |
+-------------+-----------------+---------------+
|      1      |    John Poul    |       1       |
|      2      |    Abdul S      |     NULL      |
|      3      |    Sanjay       |       1       |
+-------------+-----------------+---------------+
3 rows in set (0.02 sec)
```

You would need to do more practice to become familiar with JOINS. This is slightly a bit complex concept in MySQL/SQL and will become more clear while doing real examples.

Handling MySQL NULL Values

We have seen the SQL SELECT command along with the WHERE clause to fetch data from a MySQL table, but when we try to give a condition, which compares the field or the column value to NULL, it does not work properly.

To handle such a situation, MySQL provides three operators –

- IS NULL – This operator returns true, if the column value is NULL.
- IS NOT NULL – This operator returns true, if the column value is not NULL.
- <=> – This operator compares values, which (unlike the = operator) is true even for two NULL values.

The conditions involving NULL are special. You cannot use = NULL or != NULL to look for NULL values in columns. Such comparisons always fail because it is impossible to tell whether they are true or not. Sometimes, even NULL = NULL fails.

To look for columns that are or are not NULL, use IS NULL or IS NOT NULL.

Using NULL values at the Command Prompt

Assume that there is a table called tcount_tbl in the TUTORIALS database and it contains two columns namely tutorial_author and tutorial_count, where a NULL tutorial_count indicates that the value is unknown.

Example

Try the following examples –

```
root@host# mysql -u root -p password;
Enter password:*******

mysql> use TUTORIALS;
Database changed

mysql> create table tcount_tbl
    -> (
    -> tutorial_author varchar(40) NOT NULL,
    -> tutorial_count  INT
    -> );
Query OK, 0 rows affected (0.05 sec)

mysql> INSERT INTO tcount_tbl
    -> (tutorial_author, tutorial_count) values ('mahran', 20);

mysql> INSERT INTO tcount_tbl
    -> (tutorial_author, tutorial_count) values ('mahnaz', NULL);

mysql> INSERT INTO tcount_tbl
    -> (tutorial_author, tutorial_count) values ('Jen', NULL);

mysql> INSERT INTO tcount_tbl
    -> (tutorial_author, tutorial_count) values ('Gill', 20);

mysql> SELECT * from tcount_tbl;
```

tutorial_author	tutorial_count
mahran	20
mahnaz	NULL
Jen	NULL
Gill	20

```
+-----------------+----------------+
```
4 rows in set (0.00 sec)

mysql>

You can see that = and != do not work with NULL values as follows −

mysql> SELECT * FROM tcount_tbl WHERE tutorial_count = NULL;
Empty set (0.00 sec)

mysql> SELECT * FROM tcount_tbl WHERE tutorial_count != NULL;
Empty set (0.01 sec)

To find the records where the tutorial_count column is or is not NULL, the queries should be written as shown in the following program.

```
mysql> SELECT * FROM tcount_tbl
    -> WHERE tutorial_count IS NULL;
+-----------------+----------------+
| tutorial_author | tutorial_count |
+-----------------+----------------+
|     mahnaz      |     NULL       |
|      Jen        |     NULL       |
+-----------------+----------------+
2 rows in set (0.00 sec)
mysql> SELECT * from tcount_tbl
    -> WHERE tutorial_count IS NOT NULL;
+-----------------+----------------+
| tutorial_author | tutorial_count |
+-----------------+----------------+
|     mahran      |      20        |
|      Gill       |      20        |
+-----------------+----------------+
2 rows in set (0.00 sec)
```

Handling NULL Values in a PHP Script

You can use the if...else condition to prepare a query based on the NULL value.

Example

The following example takes the tutorial_count from outside and then compares it with the value available in the table.

```
<?php
   $dbhost = 'localhost:3036';
   $dbuser = 'root';
   $dbpass = 'rootpassword';
   $conn = mysql_connect($dbhost, $dbuser, $dbpass);

   if(! $conn ) {
      die('Could not connect: ' . mysql_error());
   }

   if( isset($tutorial_count )) {
      $sql = 'SELECT tutorial_author, tutorial_count
         FROM  tcount_tbl
         WHERE tutorial_count = $tutorial_count';
   } else {
      $sql = 'SELECT tutorial_author, tutorial_count
         FROM  tcount_tbl
         WHERE tutorial_count IS $tutorial_count';
   }

   mysql_select_db('TUTORIALS');
   $retval = mysql_query( $sql, $conn );

   if(! $retval ) {
      die('Could not get data: ' . mysql_error());
   }

   while($row = mysql_fetch_array($retval, MYSQL_ASSOC)) {
```

```php
    echo "Author:{$row['tutorial_author']}  <br> ".
    "Count: {$row['tutorial_count']} <br> ".
    "--------------------------------<br>";
  }
  echo "Fetched data successfully\n";
  mysql_close($conn);
?>
```

MySQL - Regexps

You have seen MySQL pattern matching with LIKE ...%. MySQL supports another type of pattern matching operation based on the regular expressions and the REGEXP operator. If you are aware of PHP or PERL, then it is very simple for you to understand because this matching is same like those scripting the regular expressions.

Following is the table of pattern, which can be used along with the REGEXPoperator.

Pattern	What the pattern matches
^	Beginning of string
$	End of string
.	Any single character
[...]	Any character listed between the square brackets
[^...]	Any character not listed between the square brackets
p1|p2|p3	Alternation; matches any of the patterns p1, p2, or p3

*	Zero or more instances of preceding element
+	One or more instances of preceding element
{n}	n instances of preceding element
{m,n}	m through n instances of preceding element

Examples

Now based on above table, you can device various type of SQL queries to meet your requirements. Here, I am listing a few for your understanding.

Consider we have a table called person_tbl and it is having a field called name –

Query to find all the names starting with 'st' –

mysql> SELECT name FROM person_tbl WHERE name REGEXP '^st';

Query to find all the names ending with 'ok' –

mysql> SELECT name FROM person_tbl WHERE name REGEXP 'ok$';

Query to find all the names, which contain 'mar' –

mysql> SELECT name FROM person_tbl WHERE name REGEXP 'mar';

Query to find all the names starting with a vowel and ending with 'ok' –

mysql> SELECT name FROM person_tbl WHERE name REGEXP '^[aeiou]|ok$';

MySQL - Transactions

A transaction is a sequential group of database manipulation operations, which is performed as if it were one single work unit. In other words, a transaction will never be complete unless each individual operation within the group is successful. If any operation within the transaction fails, the entire transaction will fail.

Practically, you will club many SQL queries into a group and you will execute all of them together as a part of a transaction.

Properties of Transactions

Transactions have the following four standard properties, usually referred to by the acronym ACID −

- Atomicity − This ensures that all operations within the work unit are completed successfully; otherwise, the transaction is aborted at the point of failure and previous operations are rolled back to their former state.
- Consistency − This ensures that the database properly changes states upon a successfully committed transaction.
- Isolation − This enables transactions to operate independently on and transparent to each other.
- Durability − This ensures that the result or effect of a committed transaction persists in case of a system failure.

In MySQL, the transactions begin with the statement BEGIN WORK and end with either a COMMIT or a ROLLBACK statement. The SQL commands between the beginning and ending statements form the bulk of the transaction.

COMMIT and ROLLBACK

These two keywords Commit and Rollback are mainly used for MySQL Transactions.

- When a successful transaction is completed, the COMMIT command should be issued so that the changes to all involved tables will take effect.
- If a failure occurs, a ROLLBACK command should be issued to return every table referenced in the transaction to its previous state.

You can control the behavior of a transaction by setting session variable called AUTOCOMMIT. If AUTOCOMMIT is set to 1 (the default), then each SQL statement (within a transaction or not) is considered a complete transaction and committed by default when it finishes.

When AUTOCOMMIT is set to 0, by issuing the SET AUTOCOMMIT = 0command, the subsequent series of statements acts like a transaction and no activities are committed until an explicit COMMIT statement is issued.

You can execute these SQL commands in PHP by using the mysql_query()function.

A Generic Example on Transaction

This sequence of events is independent of the programming language used. The logical path can be created in whichever language you use to create your application.

You can execute these SQL commands in PHP by using the mysql_query()function.

- Begin transaction by issuing the SQL command BEGIN WORK.
- Issue one or more SQL commands like SELECT, INSERT, UPDATE or DELETE.
- Check if there is no error and everything is according to your requirement.

- If there is any error, then issue a ROLLBACK command, otherwise issue a COMMIT command.

Transaction-Safe Table Types in MySQL

You cannot use transactions directly, but for certain exceptions you can. However, they are not safe and guaranteed. If you plan to use transactions in your MySQL programming, then you need to create your tables in a special way. There are many types of tables, which support transactions, but the most popular one is InnoDB.

Support for InnoDB tables requires a specific compilation parameter when compiling MySQL from the source. If your MySQL version does not have InnoDB support, ask your Internet Service Provider to build a version of MySQL with support for InnoDB table types or download and install the MySQL-Max Binary Distribution for Windows or Linux/UNIX and work with the table type in a development environment.

If your MySQL installation supports InnoDB tables, simply add a TYPE = InnoDB definition to the table creation statement.

For example, the following code creates an InnoDB table called tcount_tbl –

root@host# mysql -u root -p password;
Enter password:*******

mysql> use TUTORIALS;
Database changed

mysql> create table tcount_tbl
   -> (
   -> tutorial_author varchar(40) NOT NULL,
   -> tutorial_count INT
   ->) **TYPE = InnoDB**;
Query OK, 0 rows affected (0.05 sec)

For more details on InnoDB, you can click on the following link –<u>InnoDB</u>

You can use other table types like GEMINI or BDB, but it depends on your installation, whether it supports these two table types or not.

MySQL - ALTER Command

The MySQL ALTER command is very useful when you want to change a name of your table, any table field or if you want to add or delete an existing column in a table.

Let us begin with the creation of a table called testalter_tbl.

```
root@host# mysql -u root -p password;
Enter password:*******

mysql> use TUTORIALS;
Database changed

mysql> create table testalter_tbl
   -> (
   -> i INT,
   -> c CHAR(1)
   -> );
Query OK, 0 rows affected (0.05 sec)
mysql> SHOW COLUMNS FROM testalter_tbl;
+-------+---------+------+-----+---------+-------+
| Field | Type    | Null | Key | Default | Extra |
+-------+---------+------+-----+---------+-------+
| i     | int(11) | YES  |     | NULL    |       |
| c     | char(1) | YES  |     | NULL    |       |
+-------+---------+------+-----+---------+-------+
2 rows in set (0.00 sec)
```

Dropping, Adding or Repositioning a Column

if you want to drop an existing column i from the above MySQL table, then you will use the DROP clause along with the ALTER command as shown below –

mysql> ALTER TABLE testalter_tbl DROP i;

A DROP clause will not work if the column is the only one left in the table.

To add a column, use ADD and specify the column definition. The following statement restores the i column to the testalter_tbl –

mysql> ALTER TABLE testalter_tbl ADD i INT;

After issuing this statement, testalter will contain the same two columns that it had when you first created the table, but will not have the same structure. This is because there are new columns that are added to the end of the table by default. So even though i originally was the first column in mytbl, now it is the last one.

```
mysql> SHOW COLUMNS FROM testalter_tbl;
+-------+---------+------+-----+---------+-------+
| Field | Type    | Null | Key | Default | Extra |
+-------+---------+------+-----+---------+-------+
| c     | char(1) | YES  |     | NULL    |       |
| i     | int(11) | YES  |     | NULL    |       |
+-------+---------+------+-----+---------+-------+
2 rows in set (0.00 sec)
```

To indicate that you want a column at a specific position within the table, either use FIRST to make it the first column or AFTER col_name to indicate that the new column should be placed after the col_name.

Try the following ALTER TABLE statements, using SHOW COLUMNS after each one to see what effect each one has –

ALTER TABLE testalter_tbl DROP i;
ALTER TABLE testalter_tbl ADD i INT FIRST;
ALTER TABLE testalter_tbl DROP i;
ALTER TABLE testalter_tbl ADD i INT AFTER c;

The FIRST and AFTER specifiers work only with the ADD clause. This means that if you want to reposition an existing column within a table, you first must DROP it and then ADD it at the new position.

Altering (Changing) a Column Definition or a Name

To change a column's definition, use MODIFY or CHANGE clause along with the ALTER command.

For example, to change column c from CHAR(1) to CHAR(10), you can use the following command −

mysql> ALTER TABLE testalter_tbl MODIFY c CHAR(10);

With CHANGE, the syntax is a bit different. After the CHANGE keyword, you name the column you want to change, then specify the new definition, which includes the new name.

Try out the following example −

mysql> ALTER TABLE testalter_tbl CHANGE i j BIGINT;

If you now use CHANGE to convert j from BIGINT back to INT without changing the column name, the statement will be as shown below −

mysql> ALTER TABLE testalter_tbl CHANGE j j INT;

The Effect of ALTER TABLE on Null and Default Value Attributes − When you MODIFY or CHANGE a column, you can also specify whether or not the column can contain NULL values and what its default value is. In fact, if you don't do this, MySQL automatically assigns values for these attributes.

The following code block is an example, where the NOT NULL column will have the value as 100 by default.

mysql> ALTER TABLE testalter_tbl
  -> MODIFY j BIGINT NOT NULL DEFAULT 100;

If you don't use the above command, then MySQL will fill up NULL values in all the columns.

Altering (Changing) a Column's Default Value

You can change a default value for any column by using the ALTER command.

Try out the following example.

```
mysql> ALTER TABLE testalter_tbl ALTER i SET DEFAULT 1000;
mysql> SHOW COLUMNS FROM testalter_tbl;
+-------+---------+------+-----+---------+-------+
| Field | Type    | Null | Key | Default | Extra |
+-------+---------+------+-----+---------+-------+
| c     | char(1) | YES  |     | NULL    |       |
| i     | int(11) | YES  |     | 1000    |       |
+-------+---------+------+-----+---------+-------+
2 rows in set (0.00 sec)
```

You can remove the default constraint from any column by using DROP clause along with the ALTER command.

```
mysql> ALTER TABLE testalter_tbl ALTER i DROP DEFAULT;
mysql> SHOW COLUMNS FROM testalter_tbl;
+-------+---------+------+-----+---------+-------+
| Field | Type    | Null | Key | Default | Extra |
+-------+---------+------+-----+---------+-------+
| c     | char(1) | YES  |     | NULL    |       |
| i     | int(11) | YES  |     | NULL    |       |
+-------+---------+------+-----+---------+-------+
2 rows in set (0.00 sec)
```

Altering (Changing) a Table Type

You can use a table type by using the TYPE clause along with the ALTER command. Try out the following example to change the testalter_tbl to MYISAM table type.

To find out the current type of a table, use the SHOW TABLE STATUSstatement.

mysql> ALTER TABLE testalter_tbl TYPE = MYISAM;
mysql> SHOW TABLE STATUS LIKE 'testalter_tbl'\G
*************************** 1. row ***************
           Name: testalter_tbl
           Type: MyISAM
     Row_format: Fixed
           Rows: 0
 Avg_row_length: 0
    Data_length: 0
Max_data_length: 25769803775
   Index_length: 1024
      Data_free: 0
 Auto_increment: NULL
    Create_time: 2007-06-03 08:04:36
    Update_time: 2007-06-03 08:04:36
     Check_time: NULL
 Create_options:
        Comment:
1 row in set (0.00 sec)

Renaming (Altering) a Table

To rename a table, use the RENAME option of the ALTER TABLE statement.

Try out the following example to rename testalter_tbl to alter_tbl.

mysql> ALTER TABLE testalter_tbl RENAME TO alter_tbl;

You can use the ALTER command to create and drop the INDEX command on a MySQL file. We will discuss in detail about this command in the next chapter.

MySQL - INDEXES

A database index is a data structure that improves the speed of operations in a table. Indexes can be created using one or more columns, providing the basis for both rapid random lookups and efficient ordering of access to records.

While creating index, it should be taken into consideration which all columns will be used to make SQL queries and create one or more indexes on those columns.

Practically, indexes are also a type of tables, which keep primary key or index field and a pointer to each record into the actual table.

The users cannot see the indexes, they are just used to speed up queries and will be used by the Database Search Engine to locate records very fast.

The INSERT and UPDATE statements take more time on tables having indexes, whereas the SELECT statements become fast on those tables. The reason is that while doing insert or update, a database needs to insert or update the index values as well.

Simple and Unique Index

You can create a unique index on a table. A unique index means that two rows cannot have the same index value. Here is the syntax to create an Index on a table.

CREATE UNIQUE INDEX index_name
ON table_name (column1, column2,...);

You can use one or more columns to create an index.

For example, we can create an index on tutorials_tbl using tutorial_author.

CREATE UNIQUE INDEX AUTHOR_INDEX
ON tutorials_tbl (tutorial_author)

You can create a simple index on a table. Just omit the UNIQUE keyword from the query to create a simple index. A Simple index allows duplicate values in a table.

If you want to index the values in a column in a descending order, you can add the reserved word DESC after the column name.

mysql> CREATE UNIQUE INDEX AUTHOR_INDEX
ON tutorials_tbl (tutorial_author DESC)

ALTER command to add and drop INDEX

There are four types of statements for adding indexes to a table –

- ALTER TABLE tbl_name ADD PRIMARY KEY (column_list) – This statement adds a PRIMARY KEY, which means that the indexed values must be unique and cannot be NULL.
- ALTER TABLE tbl_name ADD UNIQUE index_name (column_list) – This statement creates an index for which the values must be unique (except for the NULL values, which may appear multiple times).
- ALTER TABLE tbl_name ADD INDEX index_name (column_list)– This adds an ordinary index in which any value may appear more than once.
- ALTER TABLE tbl_name ADD FULLTEXT index_name (column_list) – This creates a special FULLTEXT index that is used for text-searching purposes.

The following code block is an example to add index in an existing table.

mysql> ALTER TABLE testalter_tbl ADD INDEX (c);

You can drop any INDEX by using the DROP clause along with the ALTER command.

Try out the following example to drop the above-created index.

mysql> ALTER TABLE testalter_tbl DROP INDEX (c);

You can drop any INDEX by using the DROP clause along with the ALTER command.

ALTER Command to add and drop the PRIMARY KEY

You can add a primary key as well in the same way. But make sure the Primary Key works on columns, which are NOT NULL.

The following code block is an example to add the primary key in an existing table. This will make a column NOT NULL first and then add it as a primary key.

mysql> ALTER TABLE testalter_tbl MODIFY i INT NOT NULL;
mysql> ALTER TABLE testalter_tbl ADD PRIMARY KEY (i);

You can use the ALTER command to drop a primary key as follows −

mysql> ALTER TABLE testalter_tbl DROP PRIMARY KEY;

To drop an index that is not a PRIMARY KEY, you must specify the index name.

Displaying INDEX Information

You can use the SHOW INDEX command to list out all the indexes associated with a table. The vertical-format output (specified by \G) often is useful with this statement, to avoid a long line wraparound −

Try out the following example −

mysql> SHOW INDEX FROM *table_name*\G
....

MySQL - Temporary Tables

The temporary tables could be very useful in some cases to keep temporary data. The most important thing that should be known for temporary tables is that they will be deleted when the current client session terminates.

What are Temporary Tables?

Temporary tables were added in the MySQL Version 3.23. If you use an older version of MySQL than 3.23, you cannot use the temporary tables, but you can use Heap Tables.

As stated earlier, temporary tables will only last as long as the session is alive. If you run the code in a PHP script, the temporary table will be destroyed automatically when the script finishes executing. If you are connected to the MySQL database server through the MySQL client program, then the temporary table will exist until you close the client or manually destroy the table.

Example

The following program is an example showing you the usage of the temporary table. The same code can be used in PHP scripts using the mysql_query()function.

```
mysql> CREATE TEMPORARY TABLE SalesSummary (
   -> product_name VARCHAR(50) NOT NULL
   -> , total_sales DECIMAL(12,2) NOT NULL DEFAULT 0.00
   -> , avg_unit_price DECIMAL(7,2) NOT NULL DEFAULT 0.00
   -> , total_units_sold INT UNSIGNED NOT NULL DEFAULT 0
);
Query OK, 0 rows affected (0.00 sec)
```

```
mysql> INSERT INTO SalesSummary
    -> (product_name, total_sales, avg_unit_price, total_units_sold)
    -> VALUES
    -> ('cucumber', 100.25, 90, 2);

mysql> SELECT * FROM SalesSummary;
+--------------+-------------+----------------+------------------+
| product_name | total_sales | avg_unit_price | total_units_sold |
+--------------+-------------+----------------+------------------+
| cucumber     | 100.25      | 90.00          | 2                |
+--------------+-------------+----------------+------------------+
1 row in set (0.00 sec)
```

When you issue a SHOW TABLES command, then your temporary table would not be listed out in the list. Now, if you will log out of the MySQL session and then you will issue a SELECT command, then you will find no data available in the database. Even your temporary table will not exist.

Dropping Temporary Tables

By default, all the temporary tables are deleted by MySQL when your database connection gets terminated. Still if you want to delete them in between, then you do so by issuing the DROP TABLE command.

The following program is an example on dropping a temporary table −

```
mysql> CREATE TEMPORARY TABLE SalesSummary (
    -> product_name VARCHAR(50) NOT NULL
    -> , total_sales DECIMAL(12,2) NOT NULL DEFAULT 0.00
    -> , avg_unit_price DECIMAL(7,2) NOT NULL DEFAULT 0.00
    -> , total_units_sold INT UNSIGNED NOT NULL DEFAULT 0
);
Query OK, 0 rows affected (0.00 sec)

mysql> INSERT INTO SalesSummary
    -> (product_name, total_sales, avg_unit_price, total_units_sold)
```

```
    -> VALUES
    -> ('cucumber', 100.25, 90, 2);
```

mysql> SELECT * FROM SalesSummary;
+--------------+--------------+----------------+------------------+
| product_name | total_sales | avg_unit_price | total_units_sold |
+--------------+--------------+----------------+------------------+
| cucumber | 100.25 | 90.00 | 2 |
+--------------+--------------+----------------+------------------+
1 row in set (0.00 sec)
mysql> DROP TABLE SalesSummary;
mysql> SELECT * FROM SalesSummary;
ERROR 1146: Table 'TUTORIALS.SalesSummary' doesn't exist

MySQL - Clone Tables

There may be a situation when you need an exact copy of a table and CREATE TABLE ... SELECT doesn't suit your purposes because the copy must include the same indexes, default values and so forth.

You can handle this situation by following the steps given below −

- Use SHOW CREATE TABLE to get a CREATE TABLE statement that specifies the source table's structure, indexes and all.
- Modify the statement to change the table name to that of the clone table and execute the statement. This way, you will have the exact clone table.
- Optionally, if you need the table contents copied as well, issue an INSERT INTO ... SELECT statement, too.

Example

Try out the following example to create a clone table for tutorials_tbl.

Step 1 − Get the complete structure about the table.

```
mysql> SHOW CREATE TABLE tutorials_tbl \G;
*************************** 1. row ***************************
       Table: tutorials_tbl
Create Table: CREATE TABLE `tutorials_tbl` (
 `tutorial_id` int(11) NOT NULL auto_increment,
 `tutorial_title` varchar(100) NOT NULL default '',
 `tutorial_author` varchar(40) NOT NULL default '',
 `submission_date` date default NULL,
  PRIMARY KEY (`tutorial_id`),
  UNIQUE KEY `AUTHOR_INDEX` (`tutorial_author`)
) TYPE = MyISAM
1 row in set (0.00 sec)

ERROR:
No query specified
```

Step 2 – Rename this table and create another table.

```
mysql> CREATE TABLE clone_tbl (
  -> tutorial_id int(11) NOT NULL auto_increment,
  -> tutorial_title varchar(100) NOT NULL default '',
  -> tutorial_author varchar(40) NOT NULL default '',
  -> submission_date date default NULL,
  -> PRIMARY KEY  (tutorial_id),
  -> UNIQUE KEY AUTHOR_INDEX (tutorial_author)
-> ) TYPE = MyISAM;
Query OK, 0 rows affected (1.80 sec)
```

Step 3 – After executing step 2, you will create a clone table in your database. If you want to copy data from old table then you can do it by using INSERT INTO... SELECT statement.

```
mysql> INSERT INTO clone_tbl (tutorial_id,
    ->                        tutorial_title,
    ->                        tutorial_author,
    ->                        submission_date)
    -> SELECT tutorial_id,tutorial_title,
    ->        tutorial_author,submission_date
    -> FROM tutorials_tbl;
Query OK, 3 rows affected (0.07 sec)
Records: 3  Duplicates: 0  Warnings: 0
```

Finally, you will have an exact clone table as you wanted to have.

MySQL - Database Info

Obtaining and Using MySQL Metadata

There are three types of information, which you would like to have from MySQL.

- Information about the result of queries – This includes the number of records affected by any SELECT, UPDATE or DELETE statement.
- Information about the tables and databases – This includes information pertaining to the structure of the tables and the databases.
- Information about the MySQL server – This includes the status of the database server, version number, etc.

It is very easy to get all this information at the MySQL prompt, but while using PERL or PHP APIs, we need to call various APIs explicitly to obtain all this information.

Obtaining the Number of Rows Affected by a Query

Let is now see how to obtain this information.

PERL Example

In DBI scripts, the affected row count is returned by the do( ) or by the execute( ) command, depending on how you execute the query.

```
# Method 1
# execute $query using do( )
my $count = $dbh->do ($query);
# report 0 rows if an error occurred
printf "%d rows were affected\n", (defined ($count) ? $count : 0);

# Method 2
```

```perl
# execute query using prepare( ) plus execute( )
my $sth = $dbh->prepare ($query);
my $count = $sth->execute ( );
printf "%d rows were affected\n", (defined ($count) ? $count : 0);
```

PHP Example

In PHP, invoke the mysql_affected_rows( ) function to find out how many rows a query changed.

```php
$result_id = mysql_query ($query, $conn_id);
# report 0 rows if the query failed
$count = ($result_id ? mysql_affected_rows ($conn_id) : 0);
print ("$count rows were affected\n");
```

Listing Tablews and Databases

It is very easy to list down all the databases and the tables available with a database server. Your result may be null if you don't have the sufficient privileges.

Apart from the method which is shown in the following code block, you can use SHOW TABLES or SHOW DATABASES queries to get the list of tables or databases either in PHP or in PERL.

PERL Example

```perl
# Get all the tables available in current database.
my @tables = $dbh->tables ( );
foreach $table (@tables ){
  print "Table Name $table\n";
}
```

PHP Example

```php
<?php
  $con = mysql_connect("localhost", "userid", "password");

  if (!$con) {
    die('Could not connect: ' . mysql_error());
  }

  $db_list = mysql_list_dbs($con);

  while ($db = mysql_fetch_object($db_list)) {
    echo $db->Database . "<br />";
  }
  mysql_close($con);
?>
```

Getting Server Metadata

There are a few important commands in MySQL which can be executed either at the MySQL prompt or by using any script like PHP to get various important information about the database server.

S. No.	Command & Description
1	SELECT VERSION( ) Server version string

2   SELECT DATABASE( )

Current database name (empty if none)

3   SELECT USER( )

Current username

4   SHOW STATUS

Server status indicators

5   SHOW VARIABLES

Server configuration variables

Using MySQL Sequences

A sequence is a set of integers 1, 2, 3, ... that are generated in order on a specific demand. Sequences are frequently used in the databases because many applications require each row in a table to contain a unique value and sequences provide an easy way to generate them.

This chapter describes how to use sequences in MySQL.

Using AUTO_INCREMENT Column

The simplest way in MySQL to use Sequences is to define a column as AUTO_INCREMENT and leave the remaining things to MySQL to take care.

Example

Try out the following example. This will create table and after that it will insert few rows in this table where it is not required to give record ID because it is auto incremented by MySQL.

```
mysql> CREATE TABLE insect
    -> (
    -> id INT UNSIGNED NOT NULL AUTO_INCREMENT,
    -> PRIMARY KEY (id),
    -> name VARCHAR(30) NOT NULL, # type of insect
    -> date DATE NOT NULL, # date collected
    -> origin VARCHAR(30) NOT NULL # where collected
);
Query OK, 0 rows affected (0.02 sec)
mysql> INSERT INTO insect (id,name,date,origin) VALUES
    -> (NULL,'housefly','2001-09-10','kitchen'),
    -> (NULL,'millipede','2001-09-10','driveway'),
    -> (NULL,'grasshopper','2001-09-10','front yard');
Query OK, 3 rows affected (0.02 sec)
```

```
Records: 3  Duplicates: 0  Warnings: 0
mysql> SELECT * FROM insect ORDER BY id;
+----+-------------+------------+------------+
| id | name        | date       | origin     |
+----+-------------+------------+------------+
|  1 | housefly    | 2001-09-10 | kitchen    |
|  2 | millipede   | 2001-09-10 | driveway   |
|  3 | grasshopper | 2001-09-10 | front yard |
+----+-------------+------------+------------+
3 rows in set (0.00 sec)
```

Obtain AUTO_INCREMENT Values

The LAST_INSERT_ID( ) is a SQL function, so you can use it from within any client that understands how to issue SQL statements. Otherwise, PERL and PHP scripts provide exclusive functions to retrieve the auto incremented value of the last record.

PERL Example

Use the mysql_insertid attribute to obtain the AUTO_INCREMENT value generated by a query. This attribute is accessed through either a database handle or a statement handle, depending on how you issue the query.

The following example references it through the database handle.

```
$dbh->do ("INSERT INTO insect (name,date,origin)
VALUES('moth','2001-09-14','windowsill')");
my $seq = $dbh->{mysql_insertid};
```

PHP Example

After issuing a query that generates an AUTO_INCREMENT value, retrieve the value by calling the mysql_insert_id( ) command.

```
mysql_query ("INSERT INTO insect (name,date,origin)
VALUES('moth','2001-09-14','windowsill')", $conn_id);
$seq = mysql_insert_id ($conn_id);
```

Renumbering an Existing Sequence

There may be a case when you have deleted many records from a table and you want to re-sequence all the records. This can be done by using a simple trick, but you should be very careful to do so if your table is having joins with the other table.

If you determine that the resequencing of an AUTO_INCREMENT column is unavoidable, the way to do it is to drop the column from the table, then add it again.

The following example shows how to renumber the id values in the table using this technique.

```
mysql> ALTER TABLE insect DROP id;
mysql> ALTER TABLE insect
    -> ADD id INT UNSIGNED NOT NULL AUTO_INCREMENT FIRST,
    -> ADD PRIMARY KEY (id);
```

Starting a Sequence at a Particular Value

By default, MySQL will start sequence from 1, but you can specify any other number as well at the time of the table creation.

The following program is an example which shows how MySQL will start the sequence from 100.

```
mysql> CREATE TABLE insect
    -> (
    -> id INT UNSIGNED NOT NULL AUTO_INCREMENT = 100,
    -> PRIMARY KEY (id),
    -> name VARCHAR(30) NOT NULL, # type of insect
    -> date DATE NOT NULL, # date collected
    -> origin VARCHAR(30) NOT NULL # where collected
);
```

Alternatively, you can create the table and then set the initial sequence value with the ALTER TABLE command.

```
mysql> ALTER TABLE t AUTO_INCREMENT = 100;
```

MySQL - Handling Duplicates

Generally, tables or result sets sometimes contain duplicate records. Most of the times it is allowed but sometimes it is required to stop duplicate records. It is required to identify duplicate records and remove them from the table. This chapter will describe how to prevent the occurrence of duplicate records in a table and how to remove the already existing duplicate records.

Preventing Duplicates from Occurring in a Table

You can use a PRIMARY KEY or a UNIQUE Index on a table with the appropriate fields to stop duplicate records.

Let us take an example − The following table contains no such index or primary key, so it would allow duplicate records for first_name and last_name.

```
CREATE TABLE person_tbl (
  first_name CHAR(20),
  last_name CHAR(20),
  sex CHAR(10)
);
```

To prevent multiple records with the same first and last name values from being created in this table, add a PRIMARY KEY to its definition. When you do this, it is also necessary to declare the indexed columns to be NOT NULL, because a PRIMARY KEY does not allow NULL values −

```
CREATE TABLE person_tbl (
  first_name CHAR(20) NOT NULL,
  last_name CHAR(20) NOT NULL,
  sex CHAR(10),
  PRIMARY KEY (last_name, first_name)
);
```

The presence of a unique index in a table normally causes an error to occur if you insert a record into the table that duplicates an existing record in the column or columns that define the index.

Use the INSERT IGNORE command rather than the INSERT command. If a record doesn't duplicate an existing record, then MySQL inserts it as usual. If the record is a duplicate, then the IGNORE keyword tells MySQL to discard it silently without generating an error.

The following example does not error out and at the same time it will not insert duplicate records as well.

mysql> INSERT IGNORE INTO person_tbl (last_name, first_name)
 -> VALUES('Jay', 'Thomas');
Query OK, 1 row affected (0.00 sec)

mysql> INSERT IGNORE INTO person_tbl (last_name, first_name)
 -> VALUES('Jay', 'Thomas');
Query OK, 0 rows affected (0.00 sec)

Use the REPLACE command rather than the INSERT command. If the record is new, it is inserted just as with INSERT. If it is a duplicate, the new record replaces the old one.

mysql> REPLACE INTO person_tbl (last_name, first_name)
 -> VALUES('Ajay', 'Kumar');
Query OK, 1 row affected (0.00 sec)

mysql> REPLACE INTO person_tbl (last_name, first_name)
 -> VALUES('Ajay', 'Kumar');
Query OK, 2 rows affected (0.00 sec)

The INSERT IGNORE and REPLACE commands should be chosen as per the duplicate-handling behavior you want to effect. The INSERT IGNORE command keeps the first set of the duplicated records and discards the remaining. The REPLACE command keeps the last set of duplicates and erases out any earlier ones.

Another way to enforce uniqueness is to add a UNIQUE index rather than a PRIMARY KEY to a table.

```
CREATE TABLE person_tbl (
   first_name CHAR(20) NOT NULL,
   last_name CHAR(20) NOT NULL,
   sex CHAR(10)
   UNIQUE (last_name, first_name)
);
```

Counting and Identifying Duplicates

Following is the query to count duplicate records with first_name and last_name in a table.

```
mysql> SELECT COUNT(*) as repetitions, last_name, first_name
   -> FROM person_tbl
   -> GROUP BY last_name, first_name
   -> HAVING repetitions > 1;
```

This query will return a list of all the duplicate records in the person_tbl table. In general, to identify sets of values that are duplicated, follow the steps given below.

- Determine which columns contain the values that may be duplicated.
- List those columns in the column selection list, along with the COUNT(*).
- List the columns in the GROUP BY clause as well.
- Add a HAVING clause that eliminates the unique values by requiring the group counts to be greater than one.

Eliminating Duplicates from a Query Result

You can use the DISTINCT command along with the SELECT statement to find out unique records available in a table.

```
mysql> SELECT DISTINCT last_name, first_name
    -> FROM person_tbl
    -> ORDER BY last_name;
```

An alternative to the DISTINCT command is to add a GROUP BY clause that names the columns you are selecting. This has the effect of removing duplicates and selecting only the unique combinations of values in the specified columns.

```
mysql> SELECT last_name, first_name
    -> FROM person_tbl
    -> GROUP BY (last_name, first_name);
```

Removing Duplicates Using Table Replacement

If you have duplicate records in a table and you want to remove all the duplicate records from that table, then follow the procedure given below.

```
mysql> CREATE TABLE tmp SELECT last_name, first_name, sex
    ->         FROM person_tbl;
    ->         GROUP BY (last_name, first_name);

mysql> DROP TABLE person_tbl;
mysql> ALTER TABLE tmp RENAME TO person_tbl;
```

An easy way of removing duplicate records from a table is to add an INDEX or a PRIMARY KEY to that table. Even if this table is already available, you can use this technique to remove the duplicate records and you will be safe in future as well.

```
mysql> ALTER IGNORE TABLE person_tbl
    -> ADD PRIMARY KEY (last_name, first_name);
```

MySQL - and SQL Injection

If you take user input through a webpage and insert it into a MySQL database, there's a chance that you have left yourself wide open for a security issue known as SQL Injection. This chapter will teach you how to help prevent this from happening and help you secure your scripts and MySQL statements.

The SQL Injection usually occurs when you ask a user for input, like their name and instead of a name they give you a MySQL statement that you will unknowingly run on your database.

Never trust the data provided by a user, process this data only after validation; as a rule, this is done by pattern matching. In the following example, the username is restricted to alphanumerical characters plus underscore and to a length between 8 and 20 characters – modify these rules as needed.

```
if (preg_match("/^\w{8,20}$/", $_GET['username'], $matches)) {
   $result = mysql_query("SELECT * FROM users
              WHERE username=$matches[0]");
} else {
   echo "username not accepted";
}
```

To demonstrate this problem, consider the following excerpt.

```
// supposed input
$name = "Qadir'; DELETE FROM users;";
mysql_query("SELECT * FROM users WHERE name = '{$name}'");
```

The function call is supposed to retrieve a record from the users table, where the name column matches the name specified by the user. Under normal circumstances, $name would only contain alphanumeric characters and perhaps spaces. But here, by appending an entirely new query to $name, the call to the database turns into a disaster. The injected DELETE query removes all the records from users.

Fortunately, if you use MySQL, the mysql_query() function does not permit query stacking or executing multiple queries in a single function call. If you try to stack queries, the call fails.

However, other PHP database extensions, such as SQLite and PostgreSQL, happily perform stacked queries, executing all the queries provided in one string and creating a serious security problem.

Preventing SQL Injection

You can handle all escape characters smartly in scripting languages like PERL and PHP. The MySQL extension for PHP provides the function mysql_real_escape_string() to escape input characters that are special to MySQL.

```
if (get_magic_quotes_gpc()) {
  $name = stripslashes($name);
}

$name = mysql_real_escape_string($name);
mysql_query("SELECT * FROM users WHERE name = '{$name}'");
```

The LIKE Quandary

To address the LIKE quandary, a custom escaping mechanism must convert user-supplied % and _ characters to literals. Use addcslashes(), a function that lets you specify a character range to escape.

```
$sub = addcslashes(mysql_real_escape_string("%something_"), "%_");
// $sub == \%something\_
mysql_query("SELECT * FROM messages WHERE subject LIKE '{$sub}%'");
```

MySQL - Database Export

The simplest way of exporting a table data into a text file is by using the SELECT...INTO OUTFILE statement that exports a query result directly into a file on the server host.

Exporting Data with the SELECT ... INTO OUTFILE Statement

The syntax for this statement combines a regular SELECT command with INTO OUTFILE filename at the end. The default output format is the same as it is for the LOAD DATA command. So, the following statement exports the tutorials_tbl table into /tmp/tutorials.txt as a tab-delimited, linefeed-terminated file.

mysql> SELECT * FROM tutorials_tbl
  -> INTO OUTFILE '/tmp/tutorials.txt';

You can change the output format using various options to indicate how to quote and delimit columns and records. To export the tutorial_tbl table in a CSV format with CRLF-terminated lines, use the following code.

mysql> SELECT * FROM passwd INTO OUTFILE '/tmp/tutorials.txt'
  -> FIELDS TERMINATED BY ',' ENCLOSED BY '"'
  -> LINES TERMINATED BY '\r\n';

The SELECT ... INTO OUTFILE has the following properties −

- The output file is created directly by the MySQL server, so the filename should indicate where you want the file to be written on the server host. There is no LOCAL version of the statement analogous to the LOCAL version of LOAD DATA.
- You must have the MySQL FILE privilege to execute the SELECT ... INTO statement.

- The output file must not already exist. This prevents MySQL from clobbering files that may be important.
- You should have a login account on the server host or some way to retrieve the file from that host. Otherwise, the SELECT ... INTO OUTFILE command will most likely be of no value to you.
- Under UNIX, the file is created world readable and is owned by the MySQL server. This means that although you will be able to read the file, you may not be able to delete it.

Exporting Tables as Raw Data

The mysqldump program is used to copy or back up tables and databases. It can write the table output either as a Raw Datafile or as a set of INSERTstatements that recreate the records in the table.

To dump a table as a datafile, you must specify a --tab option that indicates the directory, where you want the MySQL server to write the file.

For example, to dump the tutorials_tbl table from the TUTORIALS database to a file in the /tmp directory, use a command as shown below.

$ mysqldump -u root -p --no-create-info \
  --tab=/tmp tutorials tutorials_tbl
password ******

Exporting Table Contents or Definitions in SQL Format

To export a table in SQL format to a file, use the command shown below.

$ mysqldump -u root -p TUTORIALS tutorials_tbl > dump.txt
password ******

This will a create file having content as shown below.

```
-- MySQL dump 8.23
--
-- Host: localhost    Database: TUTORIALS
---------------------------------------------------------
-- Server version      3.23.58

--
-- Table structure for table `tutorials_tbl`
--

CREATE TABLE tutorials_tbl (
   tutorial_id int(11) NOT NULL auto_increment,
   tutorial_title varchar(100) NOT NULL default '',
   tutorial_author varchar(40) NOT NULL default '',
   submission_date date default NULL,
   PRIMARY KEY  (tutorial_id),
   UNIQUE KEY AUTHOR_INDEX (tutorial_author)
) TYPE = MyISAM;

--
-- Dumping data for table `tutorials_tbl`
--

INSERT INTO tutorials_tbl
   VALUES (1,'Learn PHP','John Poul','2007-05-24');
INSERT INTO tutorials_tbl
   VALUES (2,'Learn MySQL','Abdul S','2007-05-24');
INSERT INTO tutorials_tbl
   VALUES (3,'JAVA Tutorial','Sanjay','2007-05-06');
```

To dump multiple tables, name them all followed by the database name argument. To dump an entire database, don't name any tables after the database as shown in the following code block.

```
$ mysqldump -u root -p TUTORIALS > database_dump.txt
password ******
```

To back up all the databases available on your host, use the following code.

```
$ mysqldump -u root -p --all-databases > database_dump.txt
password ******
```

The --all-databases option is available in the MySQL 3.23.12 version. This method can be used to implement a database backup strategy.

Copying Tables or Databases to Another Host

If you want to copy tables or databases from one MySQL server to another, then use the mysqldump with database name and table name.

Run the following command at the source host. This will dump the complete database into dump.txt file.

```
$ mysqldump -u root -p database_name table_name > dump.txt
password *****
```

You can copy complete database without using a particular table name as explained above.

Now, ftp dump.txt file on another host and use the following command. Before running this command, make sure you have created database_name on destination server.

```
$ mysql -u root -p database_name < dump.txt
password *****
```

Another way to accomplish this without using an intermediary file is to send the output of the mysqldump directly over the network to the remote MySQL server. If you can connect to both the servers from the host where the source database resides, use the following command (Make sure you have access on both the servers).

```
$ mysqldump -u root -p database_name \
   | mysql -h other-host.com database_name
```

In mysqldump, half of the command connects to the local server and writes the dump output to the pipe. The remaining half of the command connects to the remote MySQL server on the other-host.com. It reads the pipe for input and sends each statement to the other-host.com server.

MySQL - Database Import - Recovery Methods

There are two simple ways in MySQL to load data into the MySQL database from a previously backed up file.

Importing Data with LOAD DATA

MySQL provides a LOAD DATA statement that acts as a bulk data loader. Here is an example statement that reads a file dump.txt from your current directory and loads it into the table mytbl in the current database.

mysql> LOAD DATA LOCAL INFILE 'dump.txt' INTO TABLE mytbl;

- If the LOCAL keyword is not present, MySQL looks for the datafile on the server host using the looking into absolute pathname, which fully specifies the location of the file, beginning from the root of the filesystem. MySQL reads the file from the given location.
- By default, LOAD DATA assumes that datafiles contain lines that are terminated by linefeeds (newlines) and that data values within a line are separated by tabs.
- To specify a file format explicitly, use a FIELDS clause to describe the characteristics of fields within a line, and a LINES clause to specify the line-ending sequence. The following LOAD DATA statement specifies that the datafile contains values separated by colons and lines terminated by carriage returns and new line character.

mysql> LOAD DATA LOCAL INFILE 'dump.txt' INTO TABLE mytbl
 -> FIELDS TERMINATED BY ':'
 -> LINES TERMINATED BY '\r\n';

- The LOAD DATA command assumes the columns in the datafile have the same order as the columns in the table. If that is not true, you can specify a list to indicate which table columns the datafile columns should be loaded into. Suppose your table has columns a, b, and c, but successive columns in the datafile correspond to columns b, c, and a. You can load the file as shown in the following code block.

```
mysql> LOAD DATA LOCAL INFILE 'dump.txt'
  -> INTO TABLE mytbl (b, c, a);
```

Importing Data with mysqlimport

MySQL also includes a utility program named mysqlimport that acts as a wrapper around LOAD DATA, so that you can load the input files directly from the command line.

To load data from the dump.txt into mytbl, use the following command at the UNIX prompt.

```
$ mysqlimport -u root -p --local database_name dump.txt
password *****
```

If you use mysqlimport, command-line options provide the format specifiers. The mysqlimport commands that correspond to the preceding two LOAD DATA statements looks as shown in the following code block.

```
$ mysqlimport -u root -p --local --fields-terminated-by = ":" \
   --lines-terminated-by = "\r\n"  database_name dump.txt
password *****
```

The order in which you specify the options doesn't matter for mysqlimport, except that they should all precede the database name.

The mysqlimport statement uses the --columns option to specify the column order −

```
$ mysqlimport -u root -p --local --columns=b,c,a \
   database_name dump.txt
password *****
```

Handling Quotes and Special Characters

The FIELDS clause can specify other format options besides TERMINATED BY. By default, LOAD DATA assumes that values are unquoted and interprets the backslash (\) as an escape character for the special characters. To indicate the value quoting character explicitly, use the ENCLOSED BY command. MySQL will strip that character from the ends of data values during input processing. To change the default escape character, use ESCAPED BY.

When you specify ENCLOSED BY to indicate that quote characters should be stripped from data values, it is possible to include the quote character literally within data values by doubling it or by preceding it with the escape character.

For example, if the quote and escape characters are " and \, the input value "a""b\"c" will be interpreted as a"b"c.

For mysqlimport, the corresponding command-line options for specifying quote and escape values are --fields-enclosed-by and --fields-escaped-by.

Made in the USA
Monee, IL
20 June 2020

34493315R00069